The Films of
INGRID BERGMAN

The Films of
INGRID BERGMAN

_by_ LAWRENCE J. QUIRK

The Citadel Press   New York

First edition
Copyright ©1970 by Lawrence J. Quirk
All rights reserved
Published by Citadel Press, Inc.
A subsidiary of Lyle Stuart, Inc.
222 Park Avenue South, New York, N. Y. 10003
In Canada: George J. McLeod Limited
73 Bathurst St., Toronto 2B, Ontario
Printed by Mahony & Roese, Inc., New York
Manufactured in the United States of America
Designed by William Meinhardt
Library of Congress catalog card number: 72-132704
ISBN 0-8065-0212-6

This book is dedicated to the memory
of my uncles.

WILLIAM P. CONNERY, JR. (1888-1937)
U.S. Congressman from Massachusetts, 1923-1937

and

LAWRENCE J. CONNERY (1895-1941)
U.S. Congressman from Massachusetts, 1937-1941

Because in my youth they were symbols of happiness,
my memories of them run deeper than love.

Acknowledgments

Special thanks to Ernest D. Burns and Cinemabilia, New York; Mark Ricci and The Memory Shop, New York; Torsten Jungstedt and the archive staff of Filmhistoriska Samlingarna, Stockholm; Pete Sansone and United Press International, New York; Cineteca Nazionale, Centro Sperimentale di Cinematografia, Rome; the Staff of the New York Public Library's Theatre & Film Collection, Library and Museum of Performing Arts, Lincoln Center, New York; Larry Edmunds Bookshop, Hollywood; *Movie Star News*, New York; Wynn Loewenthal, Warner Bros., Inc.; John Newfield and Hortense Schorr, Columbia Pictures, Inc.; Metro-Goldwyn-Mayer, Inc.; Twentieth Century-Fox, Inc.

Also to: Margaret Connery Quirk, James E. Runyan, Frank Leyendecker, Ray Gain, Albert B. Manski, Kay Brown, Michael Greenwood, Gerald D. McDonald, Joseph L. Wilkinson, Robert Burns Gable, Richard Rheem, John and Lem Amero, Mac Lindahl, John Cocchi, Don Koll, Fred Trebel, Warren Garland, Victor Nowe, Richard W. Callahan, Kenneth G. Lawrence.

And with deep appreciation for the kindness of Miss Ingrid Bergman, who graciously loaned rare photographs from her personal files.

Contents

INGRID BERGMAN:
Her Life and Career

INGRID BERGMAN:
Her Life and Career

Like many complicated interpretive artists, Ingrid Bergman has demonstrated a colorful and at times disconcerting ambivalence in her career image and in her personal life. In her earliest years in Sweden, she was shy, self-conscious, timid, and reclusive. She was plagued with insecurities, hobbled by self-doubt, hypersensitive to internal and external influences. By eighteen, she had started to make up for lost time. And she never stopped.

The contradictory pattern of her life and career is typical of introspective, hyper-emotional souls, driven by subtle commands from an overcompensatory psyche, who swing from one extreme to another and drive themselves restlessly onward.

Miss Bergman won her first major cinematic fame as the wholesome, well-scrubbed, radiant girl with sturdy peasant strength. Soon she was playing loose women, adventuresses and trollops, and in subsequent years acquired a reputation as the *femme fatale* of the century. Prior to her adulterous 1949 involvement with the film director Roberto Rossellini and the birth of the son she bore him out of wedlock, she had been considered the most moral and exemplary of all Hollywood's married actresses—the quintessence of womanly stability and sound emotional adjustment. That was in 1948. By 1950 she had won herself a new public image that was so "notorious and scandalous" or "progressive and liberated" (depending on the predilections of the gossip) that her name was anathema among American movie exhibitors and people of conventional outlook.

The roles she played in forty-two movies, eight stage plays and four television dramas between 1934 and 1970 reflect the wide characterizational range achieved by this woman who to this day seems so uncomplicated and well-adjusted on the surface, but who is in reality one of the most psychically labyrinthine and complex creative spirits ever to grace the mediums of stage, screen and television.

In *Intermezzo, a Love Story,* the picture that brought her fame in the America of 1939, her character was sensitive, well-disposed, positive, kindly and withdrawn—all consonant with the character of an idealistic young pianist in the throes of first love. By 1941, in *Dr. Jekyll and*

With her parents, Friedel and Justus Bergman, in 1917

Mr. Hyde, she was brazen, self-destructive, erotic, hard and vulgar, as befitted a London doxy of the 1880s. But in two other 1941 films, *Rage in Heaven* and *Adam Had Four Sons,* she had gone back to wholesome virtue, in the first playing a well-meaning young wife menaced by a psychotic husband, and in the second essaying a kindly governess who must cope with the machinations of a minx, played by Susan Hayward.

In 1942's *Casablanca* she was again discovered as virtuous, well-meaning and affirmational. But in *Saratoga Trunk,* made in 1943 but released two years later, she was a saucy creole adventuress, given to brazen pursuit of men, moneyed and unmoneyed, who took her fancy. And so, on to *Spellbound,* in which she was a dedicated, disciplined, bespectacled psychiatrist softened by love for a handsome psychotic. A year later, in 1946, she was making the Hays Office nervous with *Notorious,* in which her kissing scenes with Cary Grant went on too long and too enthusiastically for the relatively prissy standards of the time.

In 1948 she was on view in two films that highlighted diametrically-opposed sides of her creative personality. *Arch of Triumph* offered her as a Parisian courtesan, drifter, and sometime singer, and *Joan of Arc* displayed her as the radiant saint whose character has gone unquestioned for five hundred years.

In 1944's *Gaslight* her sanity had been threatened by an unscrupulous husband. In 1949's *Under Capricorn* she was a dipsomaniac whose husband had assumed the blame for an old murder she had committed. She crawled into a sleeping bag with Gary Cooper for a *For Whom the Bell Tolls* love scene that had the 1943 censors wiping sweat from their brows. But that same year, in the Office of War Information release *Swedes in America,* she was blithely sharing the life of a conventional Swedish family in homespun Minnesota, complete with early-morning risings, prayers at mealtime, hayrides, and cow-milking.

The year she was seen as the mischievous Clio Dulaine of *Saratoga Trunk* had also show-

Circa 1923

ness of Henry James's *The Turn of the Screw* and the selfless, lovelorn widow of Stefan Zweig's *24 Hours in a Woman's Life*) to one "Madame Hyde" (a TV version of *Hedda Gabler*) to a combination of both—the neurotic older woman who parts via phone with a younger lover in Jean Cocteau's *The Human Voice*.

In the face of all these evidences of her creative duality, it is still remarkable that, after twenty years, people should wonder why she broke up her safe and steady life with husband and child in Hollywood to go off with Rossellini. Since she had been Jekyll-and-Hyding it in a host of pre-1949 pictures, and was also rumored to have had serious crushes on such co-stars as Spencer Tracy while conducting a largely in-absentia marriage with Dr. Peter Lindstrom, the general astonishment and, in some quarters, shocked horror with which the Rossellini involvement was greeted seems slightly ridiculous and more than slightly naive by 1970 standards. During the late 1960s the comment was mini-

At age 6, 1921

cased her, with eyes cast to Heaven and a spiritually radiant countenance, magnified a thousand times on ten thousand American screens, as the chaste, well-meaning and fussy Mother Superior of the treacly *Bells of St. Mary's*.

On the stage she had acted the role of a loving and loyal young wife of "*Liliom*" opposite Burgess Meredith in 1940. Suddenly she popped up in 1941 as the disenchanted and jaded ex-prostitute "Anna Christie." She played Joan of Arc twice on the stage—then gave herself, in *Tea and Sympathy*, to a teen-age boy to help him prove his manhood. In her three other stage presentations, "Madame Jekyll" gave way altogether to "Madame Hyde" as she essayed the bored and love-hungry wife of Turgenev's *A Month in the Country*, the wicked and destructive egoist Hedda Gabler and the domineering Deborah Harford of *More Stately Mansions*.

Her four television dramatic appearances have followed the ratio of two "Madame Jekylls" (the well-meaning though possibly psychotic gover-

15

At age 12, 1927

mal when such actresses as Julie Christie openly lived with lovers, and Mia Farrow and Vanessa Redgrave bore children out of wedlock. In these, as in other, aspects of her long and complicated career, Ingrid Bergman was a pioneer who paid an unjustly harsh penalty for blazing the trail.

In fifty-five years of intense living that was originally repressed and *internalized* and then waxed uninhibited and *externalized*, Ingrid Bergman has acquired three husbands, four children, screen careers in Sweden, Germany, France, Italy and Hollywood, solid success in all the dramatic mediums, and a romantic legend that rivals those of Isadora Duncan, Greta Garbo, Jacqueline Kennedy Onassis, Cleopatra, Madame DuBarry, Catherine the Great and the Duchess of Windsor—or, for that matter, any other startling original who comes to mind. She can walk into a room today, all delightful naturalness, well-scrubbed good looks, and understated poise; she can radiate a down-to-earth, simple, unaffected composure—and one is hard put to it to

keep in mind that here is a lady who can hold her own with the first-league legends just named —and in spades.

Many regard her as one of the great actresses of the twentieth century. Others feel that she is limited to skillful variations of a single personality-projection as against true characterizational depth. But one fact is preeminent: Ingrid Bergman never finds herself ignored.

Her pattern in childhood was typical for a burgeoning actress: she craved approval, acceptance and attention and was devastated when denied these. Doubtless there were times in Miss Bergman's latter years when she felt despairingly that she had achieved far more attention than she had bargained for—or relished.

Asked once how she managed to live with this accumulated weight of intense life experience, she replied: "I have good health—and a short memory."

Though essentially indifferent to politics, or anything else that does not relate to her imme-

With Robert Walker, Jennifer Jones, David O. Selznick, Shirley Temple, and Joseph Cotten, 1943

diate interests, she was accused of being pro-Leftist ten years ago when she pointed out publicly that many Communists were to be found on movie crews abroad and no one thought anything of it on the European sets where she had worked. She was equally candid in her opinion of certain segments of the American audience who had thumbed-down her 1961 film *Goodbye Again (Aimez-Vous Brahms?)* because in it she played an older woman in her forties having an affair with a young man of twenty-five. "Some audiences in America are still so immature and stereotyped in their thinking," she snapped. "In Europe 25-40 romantic involvements are taken as a matter of course." She has always resented the constant press reports that she was unhappy throughout her marriage to Rossellini, "when in truth for most of the time I was very happy."

Miss Bergman makes no bones about what she conceives to be the prejudiced American attitude toward the films she made with Rossellini. She feels that judgments of these films in their American release were colored by puritanical approaches to her private life rather than appraised objectively as cinematic works, and adds that much of her work with Rossellini was in her opinion ahead of its time and basically well-intentioned and sound.

Joseph Henry Steele, long her publicist and author of the 1959 book, *Ingrid Bergman: An Intimate Portrait,* regards her as "a strong woman in search of a stronger man," and after a twelve-year marriage to Dr. Lindstrom and an eight-year try with Rossellini, she seems to have found that stronger man in Swedish-born theatrical impresario Lars Schmidt, whom she married in 1958 and with whom she now lives in happy contentment outside Paris and on their private island of Danholmen off the Swedish coast.

She was born in Stockholm, Sweden, on August 29, 1915, the only child of Justus Bergman, a frustrated artist and talented painter who later opened a camera shop, and the German-born Friedel Adler, who, according to the record, was as practical and methodical as her husband was dreamy and mercurial. Her mother died when

Christmas with wounded World War II servicemen, circa 1944

Miss Bergman was only two, and her father died when she was twelve. She was then cared for by a spinster aunt—who expired suddenly in her arms of a heart attack six months later.

In other years she was to say of this period: "The days and years were filled with a terrible sense of aloneness. I became extremely shy and withdrew into a dream world of my own imagination, with creatures of fantasy who were less oppressive than the people around me. To amuse myself, I began inventing characters—villains and heroes, witches and fairies, and even animals. I made up stories as I went along, and all these characters became familiar and friendly. . . . At school my abnormal height and clumsy shyness prevented me from making friends. I barely passed from grade to grade, due partly to boredom with the regular subjects, but mostly because of my inability to stand up before the class and answer the teacher's questions. Self-

consciousness would choke the words in my throat."

With both parents and her aunt gone, the bewildered twelve-year-old orphan went to live with an elderly uncle who had five children, four of them older than her. She had never lived with other children before, and she found the negations of her life compounded tenfold. Her cousins teased her about her appearance and awkward ways. "I retreated more and more into myself," she said years later. "I determined more than ever to become an actress, because in that world of make-believe was the sanctuary I needed. I could submerge all my inhibitions and play-act at being the things I was not."

Her father had left just enough money for her to be educated privately. At the Lyceum School for Girls she learned about Joan of Arc and became obsessed with the legend of the intrepid girl who liberated France from the English. She

Studying script of 1944 radio appearance with Ronald Colman in *Death Takes a Holiday*

sought to identify herself with the warmth, idealism and gentle humor, the classical simplicity and affirmation of Joan. She also immersed herself in romantic subjects like Tristan and Isolde. As her time of graduation from the *Lycée* neared, she firmly decided on the course of her future life. Years before it had been pre-ordained: She would be an actress.

All the lonelinesses, negations and ingrown sorrows of her eighteen years now had a focus. She entered a scholarship competition at the Royal Dramatic Theatre School, one of Europe's best. Her uncle opposed the idea. He considered the theatre evil and expressed strong doubts that her gawky exterior would lend itself to such an atmosphere. She said later, "At that time one of my good faults was a tremendous stubbornness." Her continued pleas eventually wore her uncle down.

She did scenes from Rostand and Strindberg for the committee, and was one of the few selected from a hundred applicants.

At eighteen she entered for the 1933-34 term, and a few months later, met, on a blind date, a young dentist nearly a decade her senior. Peter Aron Lindstrom was his name, and even at twenty-seven he was successful at his career. His relative prosperity and sturdy enterprise impressed her. True to her life-long pattern of gravitating toward a strength she considered greater than her own (possibly a search for the

With her first husband, Dr. Peter Lindstrom

father image she had lost at twelve), she let Lindstrom take over her life completely, and sought his advice on her every move. Once she summed up the young dentist's effect on her in that early period: "It was not love at first sight, but it grew into something which, to both of us, became very important and impossible to live without."

Miss Bergman remained for a full year at the Royal Dramatic Theatre School. Her classmate, the later-famous actor Gunnar Bjornstrand, recalls her phenomenal health, strength and vitality. "Perhaps she wasn't that way underneath, but she gave the impression of total stability," Bjornstrand said, adding, "She has will power and an unbelievable memory. Learning was a snap for her."

The ever-present Lindstrom advised her to think about possible movie work, and opined that her clean good looks and radiant vitality would suit the medium very well. One day, while visiting a friend at a Swedish movie studio, she was spotted by a director, who asked her if she was interested in a film career. She said a quick yes.

The Ingrid Bergman who debuted in the 1934 Swedish film, *Munkbrogreven*, after signing a contract with Svenskfilmindustri, was on the baby-fat side but withal as wholesome and lovely a nineteen-year-old as any film-maker could wish. She also had an evident acting gift. Her role in her first film was peripheral: she was a maid in a cheap boardinghouse who tagged along as the girlfriend of a roustabout in a Bohemian-style Stockholm gang. In her second film, *Branningar,* she was a fisherman's daughter impregnated by a minister. In both films she won considerable notice, and in 1935 she was voted the most promising newcomer on the Swedish film scene. Meanwhile she had come to the attention of Gustaf Molander, one of the more talented Swedish directors of the period, and he took her on for several pictures. In each of these, under his painstaking guidance, Miss Bergman revealed an ever-burgeoning command of acting resources and personality projection.

In 1937 she married Peter Lindstrom (she called him Petter in the Swedish style) and in later years conceded that the steady tutelage of Molander and the constant encouragement of Lindstrom had aided her in developing artistically far sooner than she might otherwise have done.

Molander paired her, most notably in *Sweden-*

Receiving Oscar for *Gaslight*

hielms and *Intermezzo,* with the top male Swedish film star, Gosta Ekman; she later recalled Ekman as having been most kind and helpful, cuing her in on various acting tricks.

Her roles were varied and challenging in the ten Swedish films she made between 1934 and 1939. In *Swedenhielms* she was a rich girl who sought to marry a proud poor boy. In *Pa Solsidan* she was a bank clerk with expensive tastes who is courted by a country squire. In *Valborgsmassoafton* she was a secretary in love with an unhappily married man. The distinguished actor Lars Hanson, who earlier had appeared with Garbo in *Gösta Berling* and other films, also proved helpful and kind during their work together on the two latter films.

With her assurance developing rapidly and her good looks coming into full bloom, she was by 1936 doing such challenging parts as the love-lorn young pianist opposite Ekman in the Swed-

Visiting statue of Joan of Arc in Rheims Cathedral, France

ish version of *Intermezzo* and the scarred woman who hates the world in *En Kvinnas Ansikte*, which Joan Crawford did as *A Woman's Face* in Hollywood five years later. (In 1969 Miss Bergman, while conceding that Miss Crawford performed creditably, referred to the 1941 MGM remake with a shrug as "a more romantic version.") In *En Enda Natt* (1938) she was an upper-class girl with snobbish ideas and in *Dollar* she was a frivolous young society matron.

Meanwhile, Dr. Lindstrom had decided to undertake medical studies and began a program of work that kept the Lindstroms separated during most of the week. She has described her life at the Swedish studios in 1934-39 thus:

I enjoyed the atmosphere, the different kinds of personalities and the liveliness that was everywhere. The work itself came very easily to me. My uncle was very surprised at my success because I think he still had his doubts.

She added, significantly:

I went ahead full of confidence because in the background was always Petter. Even when I didn't see him for some time, I knew he was always there to help and advise me.

Miss Bergman had visited relatives in Germany from time to time. Always a natural linguist, she learned to speak and read German fluently, and in 1938 made one film for UFA, *Die Vier Gesellen*, in which she was one of four girls in pur-

With other 1944 Oscar winners Barry Fitzgerald and Bing Crosby

suit (with varying fortunes) of men and careers. Though the Nazis controlled the German movie industry at that time, Miss Bergman displayed her usual indifference to political matters.

Back in Sweden again, she did *Juninatten*, in which she fled from a cloddish and brutal country lover to find happiness with a gentle city boy (a reverse of the pattern then so popular in American films). In 1938 she had given birth to a daughter, whom she named Friedel Pia.

Intermezzo and *En Kvinnas Ansikte* were shown in America and Hollywood began to take an interest in her. David O. Selznick, alerted by his New York representative, Kay Brown, to Miss Bergman's singular appeal, dispatched Miss Brown to the Lindstroms in Stockholm, with the offer of a contract.

Miss Bergman and Lindstrom listened courteously to Miss Brown, but they were hesitant. Lindstrom had his medical studies to complete,

With Cary Grant and Alfred Hitchcock on the set during the filming of *Notorious*

With Roberto Rossellini and Dr. Peter Lindstrom, Hollywood, 1949

and Miss Bergman felt that Pia was too young to travel. But she had cut her teeth abroad in the one German film, on a "trial run" basis, and Hollywood represented a challenge that she did not want to forego. Eventually she and Lindstrom decided against the seven-year contract because they were not sure they wanted to leave Stockholm permanently. She did accept a one-picture deal with the proviso that if she did not register with American audiences, she would be free to return home.

With her second husband, Roberto Rossellini, circa 1953

To give her added assurance, in the face of the necessity of learning English and braving far-off Hollywood, Selznick offered to let her do a remake of *Intermezzo*. She arrived in New York in May, 1939. Miss Brown escorted her on to Hollywood, where the Selznicks took her into their home as a house guest. Selznick later said:

The minute I looked at her, I knew I had something. She had an extraordinary quality of purity and nobility and a definite star personality that is very rare. But she acted like a movie-struck teen-ager. I remember having a party for her at my home. Spencer Tracy, Charles Boyer and a dozen other movie stars were there. She just sat in a corner staring at them in awe. She was so shy she couldn't stop blushing.

Selznick inaugurated a first-class buildup for her. *Intermezzo, a Love Story*, as it was titled, was produced with painstaking care, with Leslie Howard in the Gosta Ekman role, and Gregory Ratoff directing. When Howard discovered that Miss Bergman had learned every piano note in the concerto she was to play in the film, he followed a similar program with his violin. Years later, Miss Bergman recalled with amusement that Ratoff was forever correcting her English, though his own accent was usually incomprehensible.

Ruth Roberts, an MGM English coach who had helped Hedy Lamarr and others, was assigned to tutor Miss Bergman in her lines, and though she was of Swedish descent and spoke the language fluently, Ruth Roberts did not let Miss Bergman in on it until much later. "You would have been tempted to lapse into Swedish at every opportunity, and my job was to teach you English," she said. Away from the studio, Miss Bergman worked hard with Mrs. Roberts, and with her natural flair for languages, conquered English speedily.

Intermezzo, a Love Story was released some months later, and proved an enormous success. Most of the American film critics hailed Miss Bergman's naturalness, poise, intelligence and uniquely sensitive aura. Selznick, his premonition that she would become a top Hollywood star confirmed, urged her to stay on. She told him of her long-standing ambition to play Joan of Arc and he agreed that it was a likely screen subject for her.

She returned to Sweden in the late summer of 1939. "I loved working in Hollywood," she said

Rossellini directing Miss Bergman and Marie Vitale during the filming of *Stromboli* in 1949

later, "and I liked the people I worked with. I wanted so much to come back but I had to think of my baby and Petter's studies. It all seemed so complicated."

World War II then broke out in Europe, and Lindstrom, concerned for the safety of his family, and fearful that Sweden might get involved in the war, urged her to return to America. She arrived in New York with Pia early in 1940, via steamship from Genoa. The hugely self-assured and ever-efficient Kay Brown took her in tow, and she looked forward with happy anticipation to the "Joan of Arc" film. David Selznick, who had meanwhile picked up her option, had promised her that this would be her next picture. Later Selznick saw fit to change his mind, giving as his reason that, with the war on, the historical persecution of Joan by the English would not go down well with Americans. A second disappointment came when Selznick informed her, through Kay Brown, that he had no immediate picture for her.

Miss Bergman lingered on in New York, saw all the movies and plays, and grew increasingly bored and restless in the face of continuing inactivity. She pleaded with Selznick to let her do a Broadway play, and finally he agreed. Kay Brown let it be known along the Rialto that Miss Bergman was available, and Vinton Freedley offered her the co-starring role of Julie in *Liliom*, opposite Burgess Meredith. She opened in it in March 1940 and was an instant success, with the critics praising her unaffected simplicity and warmth and her polished technique.

September, 1940, found her on loanout from Selznick to Columbia, where she played a lovable and loyal family governess in *Adam Had Four Sons*, opposite Warner Baxter. By November she was being farmed out to Metro-Goldwyn-Mayer for *Rage in Heaven*, in which she played the long-suffering young wife of psychotic Robert Montgomery. Right after that one, Miss Bergman fought for, and won, the role of Ivy in the Spencer Tracy *Dr. Jekyll and Mr. Hyde*.

She had originally been slated for the "nice-girl" role played by Lana Turner but insisted on the part of the girl of the streets who is seduced and later murdered by Hyde. "I need something I can get my teeth into," she told the powers-that-were at MGM. "Deliver me from these straight goody-goody leading ladies."

Dr. Jekyll and Mr. Hyde brought about her first professional contact with director Victor Fleming, the leonine, masterful man who had guided *Gone With the Wind*. Seven years later he would direct her in the filming of the long-deferred *Joan of Arc*. Fleming called her "Angel," and she told friends that he had given her enormous creative inspiration. She also found Spencer Tracy inspiring, and he too proved helpful and cooperative. There were rumors that Tracy and Bergman had fallen in love during the shooting, but whatever the truth, they did not further the relationship on other than a friendly basis once the picture was completed. Since it was known that Miss Bergman was apt to get starry-eyed, however innocently, about most of her leading men, the involvement, if such it was, did not create much of a flurry. Tracy had not wanted to do the film, feeling that he was miscast, and his instinct about the role was confirmed when the critics roasted him and handed most of the acting kudoes to Miss Bergman, who was electric and sensuously kinetic as the fallen woman. *Dr. Jekyll and Mr. Hyde* established once and for all that she was an actress of considerable versatility and range and could be as convincing in the projection of evil as when she was radiating sweetness and light.

About this time, Dr. Lindstrom joined his wife and child in America. He resumed his medical studies, this time at the University of Rochester. Miss Bergman, he and Pia found a house in that upstate New York community, and she tried to adjust herself to the amenities of domestic life. But she found Rochester excruciatingly dull. The only social life she knew was among the doctor's medical associates who, naturally enough, talked medicine all night. Bored and restless, she went off to New York to visit her sterling, ever-welcoming friend Kay Brown. Again she wandered the streets of Manhattan visiting theatres and museums that spring of 1941. Her two latest films had opened with flattering reviews for her personal contribution, and with her American audience growing, she began again to hound Selznick for parts—any parts.

"It's awful to sit around for months trying to find something to do," she said of this period in her life. "I couldn't understand the reason for these long layoffs. David Selznick was too fussy; nothing was good enough. Either the story wasn't right for me or the part wasn't big enough. I didn't care how short the part was as long as it was good."

Eventually worn down by her demands, Selznick staged a production of *Anna Christie* at Santa Barbara's Lobero Theatre and put Miss Bergman into the title role. The play opened in August, 1941, and later played in San Francisco and Maplewood, New Jersey. While she gave a technically expert performance, some critics declared that she seemed too much the "good

Touring Etruscan ruins with Rossellini, 1949

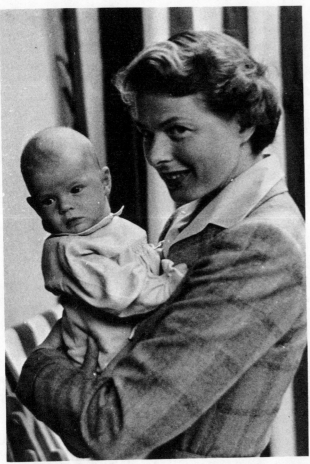

With her son Robertino, 1950

woman" to successfully approximate the jaded bitterness and despair of the ex-prostitute Anna who tries to find a haven with her father and a second chance at love.

Back again in Rochester, Miss Bergman languished briefly, then took her child back to Hollywood. She resumed her English studies with Ruth Roberts, kept track of most of the movies being released, sometimes looking at four or five in a day, and when Paramount in 1942 purchased the screen rights to Ernest Hemingway's *For Whom the Bell Tolls,* she read the book and pressured Selznick to help her get the role. Selznick agreed that the part would be a plum, and he in turn pressured Paramount. But the studio had other ideas, and told him that Miss Bergman did not fit their conception of the war-weary, spirit-wounded Maria. Other actresses were under consideration, including Olivia de Havilland and Joan Fontaine. Finally Paramount decided on Vera Zorina, who had had a brief prior film career, but was better known as a ballerina. This though Selznick had asked Hemingway to endorse Miss Bergman for the role and the author and the ambitious actress had been photographed together, with Hemingway according her his well-publicized blessing.

Deeply disappointed, Miss Bergman con-

Versatile Miss Bergman shows off her talents as a magician, doing a card trick at a gala benefit performance of a Paris circus, 1957

Receiving congratulatory telegrams in Paris after winning 1956 Oscar for *Anastasia*

has a brief romance with Gary Cooper's idealistic Robert Jordan, fighter for the loyalist cause in the Spanish Civil War. The picture, however, garnered a great deal of public attention and despite the flaws that some critics discerned in her screen image in this part, her acting won her an Academy Award nomination, just as Selznick had predicted it would.

During World War II, Miss Bergman made a number of war bond tours and visited military installations entertaining the troops. She even made a film for the Office of War Information, *Swedes in America*, depicting the lives of Swedish-Americans in Minnesota. The film was shown in Sweden and later in England. In the summer of 1945, after V-E Day, Miss Bergman toured army camps in Germany, taking along with her a script about Joan of Arc, excerpts from which she read to the soldiers, while filling in for them descriptions of scenes and situations. She even found time for a radio appearance in 1944, opposite Ronald Colman in *Death Takes a Holiday*.

In late 1943 she began work on *Gaslight*, opposite Charles Boyer, again on loan to Metro-Goldwyn-Mayer. As the fear-maddened wife whose scheming husband deliberately tries to drive her insane, Miss Bergman projected so much emotional power and interpretive mesmerism that it won her the 1944 Academy Award.

She was then seen in three pictures, released close together in the 1945-1946 season, whose cumulative impact metamorphosed her into one of Hollywood's superstars. These were: *Spellbound*, the last of her films to be personally produced by Selznick; *The Bells of St. Mary's*, on loanout to RKO, in which she played a nun opposite Bing Crosby's priest in a sort of *Going My Way* sequel (she had hounded Selznick persistently to let her play it); and *Saratoga Trunk*.

The last-named film had a rather odd history. Made in February-May, 1943, it was shown around the army camps overseas for two years, and its theatrical release was delayed to late 1945. It did not go into general release until early in 1946, in accordance with Warners' unique policy (applied to a number of their films) of holding up releases of pictures for several years in order to catch the right post-war mood of the public. *Saratoga Trunk* was colorful period stuff, based on an Edna Ferber novel, and Miss Bergman was flashy and vivacious as a creole adventuress opposite Gary Cooper's Texas gambler.

tinued her search for the right story. Selznick, equally alert at this time, persuaded her to go along with a loanout to Warners for *Casablanca*, opposite Humphrey Bogart—and the picture made her a star of the first rank. As Elsa, torn between her love for the adventurous cabaret owner, Rick, and loyalty to her underground leader husband, Miss Bergman registered as so warm, radiant and cinematically exciting that the critics went all out. The film itself was one of the biggest critical and popular hits of its year.

Another lucky break then came her way. Soon after shooting began on *For Whom the Bell Tolls*, Paramount decided that Vera Zorina was not right for Maria after all, and Miss Bergman was handed the role she had coveted. When the picture came out in the summer of 1943, there were mixed critical reactions to her work, some of it commenting on her essential unsuitability for the part of the life-battered Spanish girl who

Holding New York Film Critics' award for *Anastasia*. Kirk Douglas holds his for *Lust For Life*.

The last picture due under her old Selznick contract was *Notorious* in which she was teamed with Cary Grant. It was directed by Alfred Hitchcock for RKO and released in the fall of 1946. Dr. Lindstrom had permanently settled with her in Hollywood, and he and Miss Bergman came to feel that Selznick had been making too much money out of her via loanouts and that she had not been sufficiently remunerated for her services. The record seems to bear this out, for Miss Bergman at the time was earning about $80,000 a year ($2000 per week, forty weeks each year). On the other hand, Selznick had gotten $125,000 from Warners for the *Casablanca* loanout, $150,000 from Paramount for *For Whom the Bell Tolls* and $175,000 from RKO for *The Bells of St. Mary's*. The last deal had also included the remake rights for *Little Women* and *A Bill of Divorcement* and the loan to Selznick of an ace RKO director whose services he coveted. More-

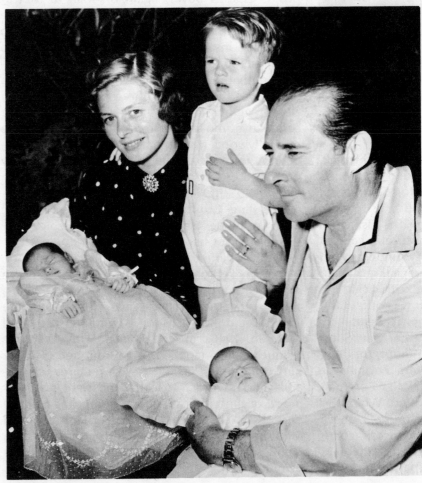

With baby daughters Ingrid Isotta and Isabella, Robertino and Roberto Rossellini. Rome, 1952.

over, the Lindstroms allegedly felt that Selznick was favoring Jennifer Jones with the choicer assignments. (Selznick and Miss Jones were later married.)

Meanwhile rumors that all was not idyllic in the Bergman-Lindstrom marriage kept circulating. The career separations had been extensive over the years. Reports that Miss Bergman was infatuated with this or that actor or director were constant. Lewis Milestone, who directed her in *Arch of Triumph*, opined: "Lindstrom had old-fashioned European ideas. He took the attitude that he had bestowed his name on a poor orphan girl and therefore she should be grateful to him for the rest of her life. There were implications all the time. . . . He was the solid citizen who had rescued a poor waif. He never let her forget it. But how long can you operate on gratitude?"

Carrying her twins, 1952

The couple had gradually drifted apart in other ways. Lindstrom preferred the company of medicos and liked a quiet, study-filled life. Miss Bergman craved glamor and excitement and the hearty hurly-burly and stimulating encounters of show business. She chafed under the necessity of conforming to Lindstrom's rigid Scandinavian ideas of domesticity and the subservience of wife to husband in matters great and small. She was, however, appreciative of her husband's strengths, and went along with his suggestion that he manage her career. When the Selznick contract expired, the Lindstroms refused to sign another and struck out on their own.

The decision proved unwise. For all his Nordic steadiness, practicality and reliability, Lindstrom lacked a feel for story values or show business gambles that paid off. The shrewd trading instinct and admirable common sense that had

The Rossellinis with Rossellini's son Renzo, right, from his previous marriage. Italy, 1953.

29

Boyer, Miss Bergman got $175,000 in cash and twenty-five per cent of the net profits. The film was produced by a new company, Enterprise Pictures, headed by Charles Einfeld and David Loew, and the profits were nil. Instead, a $2,000,000 loss was sustained. Critics complained that the spirit of the Erich Maria Remarque novel about refugees from Nazism in 1938 Paris had been lost, and that the love scenes between Bergman and Boyer went on forever.

While making the film, Miss Bergman asked her husband for a divorce, but later they were reconciled. Years afterward, she reminisced:

In 1947 I had everything that a woman could expect in life. I was a big star, I had a lovely daughter and a nice husband. We didn't love each other any more, but many marriages are like this and they endure. I had a beautiful house and of course a swimming pool. I remember one day sitting at the pool and suddenly the tears were streaming down my cheeks. Why was I so unhappy? I had success. I had security. But it wasn't enough. I was exploding inside.

made him so helpful to his wife in her Swedish film period deserted him in the more confusing, mercurial Hollywood atmosphere, according to most reports.

For *Arch of Triumph*, again opposite Charles

Curtsying to King Gustaf VI of Sweden at Stockholm opening night, 1959. Lars Schmidt is at right, behind the king. In foreground, Queen Louise.

Holding her Golden David film award. Rome, 1957.

She had meanwhile achieved a signal stage triumph in *Joan of Lorraine,* which opened on Broadway in the fall of 1946. The critics paid tribute to her radiance and authority and essential rightness in the part. Impulsively she told friends that she was through with films and that the stage would henceforth be her life. But a few months later she was restless again and back in Hollywood.

Her next project was the film version of *Joan of Arc,* made by a corporation consisting of Miss Bergman, Lindstrom and Walter Wanger. The last-named headed the group and made a heavy financial investment. The film cost $5,000,000, drew mixed reactions from American critics, and proved a resounding financial failure. Miss Bergman insisted for years afterward that the film had not won the appreciation it deserved in America and that it had gotten a kinder recep-

tion in European quarters. She also feels that the film's over-all quality was better than was realized at the time—and there are grounds for believing that what she says is true.

Meanwhile, the 1947-48 reconciliation with Lindstrom wasn't taking. She began to lose faith in her husband's decisions about her career; her dissatisfaction and ennui increased. She had formed a good friendship with brilliant photographer Robert Capa, who talked much of the cinematic exploits of the Italian film director Roberto Rossellini, then forty-three. Father of the postwar Italian neo-realistic school of films, Rossellini had created a sensation with *Open City* and *Paisan.* Miss Bergman saw *Open City* and was impressed by its raw, grainy realism. For some time she had expressed herself to friends as dissatisfied with Hollywood's overly commercial emphasis. "I'd rather be remembered for one

With Cary Grant in London during *Indiscreet* press conference, 1957

great artistic film than all my money-making hits," she declared. She then went to see another Rossellini film *(Paisan)* in early 1948, and found herself so galvanized that she sat down and wrote the famous "Ti Amo" letter to the director.

It went:

I saw your films *Open City* and *Paisan* and enjoyed them very much. If you need a Swedish actress who speaks English very well, who has not forgotten her German,

The young Rossellinis with their mother during shooting of *The Visit, 1964*

who is not very understandable in French and who in Italian knows only "Ti Amo," I am ready to come and make a film with you. Best regards, Ingrid Bergman.

Rossellini cabled back:

I HAVE JUST RECEIVED WITH GREAT EMOTION YOUR LETTER WHICH HAPPENS TO ARRIVE ON THE ANNIVERSARY OF MY BIRTHDAY ON THE MOST PRECIOUS GIFT STOP IT IS ABSOLUTELY TRUE THAT I DREAMED OF MAKING A FILM WITH YOU AND FROM THIS VERY MOMENT I WILL DO EVERYTHING THAT SUCH A DREAM BECOMES REALITY AS SOON AS POSSIBLE STOP I WILL WRITE YOU A LONG LETTER TO SUBMIT TO YOU MY IDEAS STOP WITH MY ADMIRATION PLEASE ACCEPT THE EXPRESSION OF MY GRATITUDE TOGETHER WITH MY BEST REGARDS.

In the summer of 1948 Miss Bergman went to England to make *Under Capricorn* with Alfred Hitchcock. The role of an 1831-style Australian dipsomaniac with a murder in her past was unsuited to her and the usual expert Hitchcock touches were largely absent. This picture likewise failed with critics and public, and three failures in a row conclusively shook her confidence in the current course of her life and ca-reer. She was ready for a change, but no one then dreamed how sweeping and all-embracing that change would be.

During the making of the Hitchcock film, she met Rossellini in Paris. She, her husband, and Rossellini set up an arrangement to produce *Stromboli* in Italy. Howard Hughes, who had taken over RKO, provided the financing. In early 1949 Rossellini joined Miss Bergman and Lindstrom in Hollywood for further discussions on *Stromboli*, and Rossellini and Bergman got to know each other better. He returned to Rome in February, Miss Bergman followed in March, and production began on the notorious and ill-fated film.

Soon rumors of a love affair between the actress and the Italian director were spreading in the European and American press, and the film location was besieged by reporters and photographers. A friend, Michel Bernheim, said later, "She thought Rossellini would be a great director for her. He was the new strong man in her life. She was looking for someone to look up to and really admire."

Friends and relatives of both parties were soon expressing disapproval of the affair. Her support-

With her children in Wales in 1958 during work on *Inn of the Sixth Happiness*

With husband Lars Schmidt in Wales, 1958

ers felt that Rossellini was taking advantage of her loneliness and restless desire for change and excitement, and his cohorts opined that Miss Bergman was taking him away from the kind of film he did best and forcing him into an uneasy blend of realism and commercial pap. Whatever the truth of the matter, *Stromboli*, badly edited by Hollywood cutters who sought to head off

Breen Office censorship, was an utter failure. Rossellini insisted that the editing had snipped the guts out of the picture.

In the same month that saw the release of *Stromboli* (February, 1950), Miss Bergman gave birth to a baby boy, Robertino, in a Rome clinic. Italian gendarmes were placed before her door to keep out the hordes of reporters and curiosity-seekers. The news of her pregnancy had been broken by Louella Parsons in December, 1949, and the scandal that erupted assumed major proportions. Miss Bergman was called an adulteress and a wicked woman, and denounced on the floor of Congress. Sanctions were demanded against her future pictures. Never did a major star fall more completely from grace more swiftly, at least in America.

Afterward David O. Selznick publicly admitted:

I'm afraid I'm responsible for the public's image of her as Saint Ingrid. I hired a press agent who was an expert at shielding stars from the press, and we released only stories that emphasized her sterling character. We deliberately built her up as the normal, healthy, non-neurotic career woman devoid of scandal and with an idyllic home life. I guess that backfired later.

Miss Bergman herself commented: "People didn't expect me to have emotions like other women."

A week after her son was born, Miss Bergman

More **Bergman** versatility. She takes on director Anthony Asquith's dare on set of *The Yellow Rolls-Royce* in London, performing the difficult tablecloth trick. Above, she begins to pull off tablecloth without disturbing articles on top.

She clutches the tablecloth, as a matador might, after performing the trick, using a technique she learned as a child.

filed suit for divorce against Dr. Lindstrom. Then in May she underwent a proxy marriage to Rossellini in Juarez, Mexico. In California, Dr. Lindstrom sued for a divorce and secured it. He kept Pia, then twelve, with him and tried to prevent his wife from retaining any influence over the child. Two years later Miss Bergman asked the California courts to force her first husband to allow Pia, who had meanwhile been renamed Jenny Ann, to visit her in Italy. The petition was denied. Jenny Ann told the court she liked her mother but did not love her, and that she wanted to remain with her father. In later years, mother and daughter were reconciled, but the separation from Jenny Ann caused Miss Bergman considerable anguish.

Some years later Miss Bergman told a reporter that she didn't mind paying like a good sport for her mistakes, but she didn't feel it was right that her children should pay for them, too.

During 1950 and 1951 the Rossellini-Bergman thing continued to be the *pièce de résistance* of the international gossip and scandal sheets, but when Miss Bergman's twin daughters Isabella

Triumph lights her face as she wins bet with Asquith. (Her method? Place sheet of cellophane over the tablecloth but under the dishes. China, glass and silver adhere to cellophane, but cloth does not. But it still involves considerable dexterity!)

With the Rossellini children and Pia Lindstrom, child of her first marriage, in her dressing room after stage performance of *More Stately Mansions*, New York, 1967

and Isotta were born in June, 1952, the dust began to settle and the Bergman reputation started a long uphill climb to a more respectable aura.

Meanwhile Miss Bergman and Rossellini embarked on a series of films that were badly received. These included: *Europa '51 (The Greatest Love)* in which the star portrayed an idealist who goes mad; *We, the Women (Siamo Donne)* an episode film in which she played a flighty actress at war with a rose-gobbling chicken, as directed by Rossellini; *Viaggio in Italia (Strangers)* opposite George Sanders, in which she played an English matron who reconciles with her husband (Sanders) during an Italian journey; and *Fear*, made in Germany opposite Mathias Wiemann, in which Miss Bergman was an adulterous wife who submits to blackmail.

As regards the Rossellini film period of her career, Miss Bergman has consistently maintained that the films suffered because of the then-current prejudices against her and Rossellini, and that they were ahead of their time and much better than they were originally credited as being, especially when free of censorial tampering. "The press," she said in 1969, "kept insisting how unhappy I was in that period (1950-1953)

With husband Lars Schmidt and daughter Pia Lindstrom on opening night of play, *More Stately Mansions*, 1967

when actually I was very happy." Rossellini had a large circle of friends from all walks of Italian life, and Miss Bergman enjoyed the lively gatherings in their Rome apartment.

However, the failure of their films together and their problems with *Joan of Arc at the Stake*, which Miss Bergman starred in and Rossellini staged in a number of European cities, brought

Reminiscing with Alfred Hitchcock, 1967

them to the end of their financial and career tethers by 1955. Debts were piling up, Rossellini out of pride refused to let Miss Bergman do films for other producers, though she had some good offers, and adverse press reaction to *Joan of Arc at the Stake* in Sweden and elsewhere proved discouraging.

One of Rossellini's friends maintained at this time that the director's neo-realistic techniques and his famous habit of shooting a film spontaneously as he went along, without benefit of script, conflicted with Miss Bergman's Hollywood-oriented approach to film-making.

In 1955 Miss Bergman, tired of being broke, and convinced that she would never make a successful film with Rossellini, overruled his objections and did *Paris Does Strange Things* for her friend Jean Renoir in Paris. The following year she agreed to do *Tea and Sympathy* on the Paris stage. Rossellini called the play "trash," sulked in her dressing room during the wild plaudits on opening night, and went off to India to make documentary films. Shortly afterward, Kay Brown arrived from America with a 20th Century-Fox offer of the title role in their forthcoming production *Anastasia,* about the Czar's daughter who supposedly had escaped the 1918 mass murder of the Russian Imperial Family.

20th Century-Fox at this time made known its

feeling that Miss Bergman had outlived and faced down the public feeling in America against her to the point where the risk of starring her in an expensive, U.S.-distributed film was worth taking. *Anastasia* proved highly successful, and won Miss Bergman her second Academy Award.

By 1957 she was forced to face the fact that her marriage to Rossellini had foundered hopelessly. When the director returned from India with Sonali Das Gupta, wife of an Indian film director, and Das Gupta shortly thereafter gave birth to Rossellini's daughter, Miss Bergman and the director set annulment proceedings in motion in Italy on the ground that her divorce from Lindstrom had never been registered in Sweden.

Later Miss Bergman said of the Rossellini annulment: "If only Roberto had accomplished something successfully, the marriage might have been saved. I understood him, but I was powerless to alter the way things were. Roberto's pride was hurt. Everything seemed to go against him—very hard for a man of his talent and ability to swallow. And *Anastasia* and *Tea and Sympathy* didn't help any."

In 1958 Kay Brown introduced Miss Bergman to Lars Schmidt, a theatrical impresario from a wealthy Swedish shipping family. They found that they had much in common and began going out together. They soon discovered that they

After presenting Oscar to Barbra Streisand, Hollywood, 1969

girls are eighteen. The separate apartment for the children represents a compromise between Miss Bergman and Rossellini on the children's upbringing and way of life. Jenny Ann, now thirty-two, went through a short-lived marriage some years ago and has since tried movie acting. As Pia Lindstrom, she is now a successful TV news reporter and commentator. These days she sees her mother relatively often. Rossellini's career enjoyed a short-lived upsurge with pictures like *General Della Rovere* in 1960, but he has yet to repeat the major successes of his floodtide years. Dr. Lindstrom remarried and had a son by that marriage and in recent years has won a steadily growing reputation as a brain surgeon.

Since the ill-fated *Paris Does Strange Things* in 1957, a confused trifle badly edited for American release, Miss Bergman has done *Indiscreet* (1958), a delightful comedy with Cary Grant, and *The Inn of the Sixth Happiness* (1958), in which she played an Englishwoman who becomes a missionary in China. *Goodbye Again* (1961), with Yves Montand and Anthony Perkins, was shot in Paris and concerned a forty-year-old woman torn between an older and younger man. *The Visit* (1964), the screen version of the Friedrich Duerrenmatt play about the wealthy woman who returned to a mid-European village seeking revenge on a man who had betrayed her years before, co-starred Miss Bergman and Anthony Quinn. In *The Yellow Rolls-Royce* a three-episode film released by MGM in 1965, Miss Bergman shared Episode III with Omar Sharif and portrayed a wealthy American who helps a Yugoslav partisan to fight the Nazis in 1941. She did another episode segment in *Stimulantia*, her first Swedish film in twenty-five years. It was directed in 1964 by her old mentor, Gustaf Molander, and co-starred her with her old schoolmate at the Royal Dramatic Theatre School, Gunnar Bjornstrand, in a segment based on De Maupassant's "The Necklace." The story concerned a couple who spend years paying for a necklace borrowed by the wife and lost, only to discover it was worthless paste. This film, as yet unreleased in America, played in Sweden in 1967.

Recently she did two films in America for Columbia Pictures. The first was *Cactus Flower*, in which she again demonstrated her sharp comedy timing in the role of a dental nurse who wins the dentist from a beautiful young kook. Lauren Bacall had played the role in the Broadway hit. After this she did *A Walk in the Spring*

were in love, and Miss Brown found herself receiving regular telegrams from Miss Bergman and Schmidt with "Thank You" on them. Schmidt is said to resemble Lindstrom more than Rossellini in character and temperament, but he offers Miss Bergman, as neither of his predecessors did, the right combination of strength, solicitude and flexibility that exactly approximates the pattern she had long sought in a husband.

From the time she married Schmidt in December, 1958, Miss Bergman has enjoyed a relatively serene and uneventful private life. Schmidt has excellent business judgment and also advises her in career matters. Over the past twelve years, Miss Bergman has done only eight films, but she has been fairly active on the stage and on TV. She spaces out her assignments, enjoys watching her children grow and spends much time with them and her husband on their Swedish island of Danholmen and at their country house near Paris.

Miss Bergman regularly visits her children in Italy. They maintain their own apartment in Rome, under the care of a housekeeper. Robertino, called Robin, is now twenty and the twin

With her *Anastasia* co-star, Helen Hayes, in 1967

Rain, a 1970 release in which she plays a middle-aged wife of a university professor who falls in love with an earthy Tennesseean, Anthony Quinn, but leaves him reluctantly to resume her former life.

On television she has been seen in *The Turn of the Screw* (1959), *24 Hours in a Woman's Life* (1961), *Hedda Gabler* (1963), and *The Human Voice* (1967). She did Ibsen's *Hedda Gabler* on the Paris stage in 1962; Turgenev's *A Month in the Country* with Michael Redgrave in England in 1965, and Eugene O'Neill's *More Stately Mansions* in Los Angeles and New York in 1967. Her acting in all four television dramas was lavishly praised, though the vehicles themselves varied in quality.

The verdict on her stage and TV versions of *Hedda Gabler* seems to have been that she was obviously too beneficent-spirited a person to do full justice to Ibsen's vindictive and complex heroine. She got good notices as the love-obsessed and lonely Natalia in *A Month in the Country* in London after a hesitant out-of-town

summer engagement at Guildford, and her beauty and charm were praised in her role of the domineering matriarch in *More Stately Mansions,* although Colleen Dewhurst garnered more acting kudos.

In 1969 Miss Bergman told a Hollywood columnist: "I don't fight the years. Every woman, and I include myself, feels a little sad over the thought of growing old when the wrinkles show up around the eyes and on the neck. It's demoralizing. I've never had my face lifted. But that doesn't mean I haven't thought about it." She added: "The best way to keep young is to keep going in whatever it is that keeps you going. With me that's work, and a lot of it. And when a job is finished, relax and have fun."

Concerning her latest film, *A Walk in the Spring Rain,* she told *The New York Times:*

It is a warm, gentle story...it shows a woman's awakening to love and to the natural world around her. Also, it is about mature people. Today everything is youth, youth.

Basket-lunching with Frank Leyendecker of *Greater Amusements* (left) and other film press representatives during New York location-shooting of *A Walk in the Spring Rain*, 1969

Older people must feel rather neglected. This film shows that a woman fifty years old can fall in love and feel like a young girl. . . . There are so many ugly, horrible movies today with violence and obvious nudity, and all the brutality. I get so many scripts over the years; I would read them and turn them down, and then someone else would make the picture and I would read the reviews and think, "Ah, I'm glad I didn't do it."

Goldie Hawn, the young actress who appeared with Miss Bergman in *Cactus Flower*, in the course of which the twenty-three-year-old and the fifty-four-year-old did a frantic bugaloo together in a discotheque, said of her: "Oh, but she's a woman's woman. I mean, she is everything a woman should be. She's the kind of woman men aren't afraid of because she's so warm. She has a regal quality. It's too bad she isn't a queen of some country."

After all the *sturm und drang* of a life lived to the fullest, and the blessings and damnings that inevitably attend a many-sided, intense pattern of existence, Miss Bergman, at fifty-five, can take comfort from the fact that a great many people, circa 1970, share Miss Hawn's opinion of her.

The Swedish Period

Munkbrogreven

(The Count of the Monk's Bridge)

Svenskfilmindustri, 1934

CAST

Valdemar Dahlquist, Sigurd Wallen, Eric Abrahamson, Weyler Hildebrand, Artur Cederborg, Edvin Adolphson, Ingrid Bergman, Tollie Zellman, Julia Caesar, Arthur Fischer, Emil Fjellstrom, Viktor "Kulorten" Andersson.

CREDITS

Produced by AB Fribergs Filmbyra. Directed by Edvin Adolphson and Sigurd Wallen. Screenplay by Gosta Stevens from the play Greven fran Gamla Sta'n by Arthur and Sigfried Fischer. Photographed by Ake Dahlquist. Music by Jules Sylvain. Edited by Rolf Husberg. Premiere, Skandia Theatre, Stockholm, January 21, 1935. Length, 2341 meters.

THE STORY

In Stockholm's "Old Town," "The Count of the Monk's Bridge" (Valdemar Dahlquist) a good-natured roustabout and petty larcenist, leads a group of his raffish, non-conformist friends on an all-day binge. They down morning beers near the monk's bridge, go on to flop joints, try to evade the stringent liquor-rationing laws, visit the flea market, then end up in a wild chase in which they successfully evade the police. The plot is almost non-existent; it is merely the recital of a day in the life of free Bohemian spirits, and in another sense a travelogue-style tour of Stockholm's more colorful Bohemian dis-

With Edvin Adolphson

43

the doings of the romantic lovebirds. The latter is a refreshing and straightforward young lady, sunny of spirit, self-assured, altogether an asset to the film.

In Folkets Dagblad (Swedish):

The film has every chance to become a box-office smash. An important contribution to this is made by the group of actors. . . . Young Miss Bergman [is] a somewhat overweight copy of Birgit Tengroth, with an unusual way of speaking her lines.

In Stockholms-Tidningen (Swedish):

Beautiful photography. . . . Svenskfilmindustri as usual proves its brilliance through superb technique. . . . Ingrid Bergman is hefty and sure of herself.

trict, circa 1934. All of the action takes place while the liquor-thirsty members of the group attempt to keep just one jump ahead of the constabulary, which makes every effort to catch them but does not succeed. A 1930s-style Swedish attempt to imitate Mack Sennett capers and chases, with much comedy of the tomfoolery type, the film ends at sundown. Miss Bergman, in this her first film, plays Elsa, a maid in a cheap hotel, who is the love interest of Ake *(Edvin Adolphson),* one of the merrymakers. Her role was largely peripheral.

REVIEWS

In Svenska Dagbladet (Swedish):

A good movie, much better than a slew of other popular Swedish films. . . . The picture also offers a debut, that of Ingrid Bergman. She is a beautiful and statuesque girl.

In Social-Demokraten (Swedish):

Edvin Adolphson and Ingrid Bergman handle

Branníngar

(Ocean Breakers)

Svenskfilmindustri, 1935

CAST

Tore Svennberg, Sten Lindgren, Carl Strom, Ingrid Bergman, Bror Ohlsson, Knut Frankman, Carin Swenson, Weyler Hildebrand, Georg Skarstedt, Henning Ohlsson, Vera Lindby, Viktor Ost, Emmy Albiin, Viktor Andersson, Helga Brofeldt, Carl Browallius, Olle Grenberg, Holger Lowenadler, E. Rosen.

CREDITS

Produced by Film AB Skandinavien. Directed by Ivar Johansson. Screenplay by Ivar Johansson from an idea by Henning Ohlssen. Photographed by Julius Jaenzon. Music arranged by Eric Bengtsson. Premiere, Palladium, Stockholm, February 22, 1935. Length, 1916 meters.

THE STORY

Daniel Nordeman *(Sten Lindgren)* has been forced to become a minister, though he lacks a true vocation. During a night of storm, after his second sermon, he looks upon Karin Ingman *(Ingrid Bergman)* daughter of a fisherman *(Carl*

With Sten Lindgren

In *Svenska Dagbladet* (Swedish):

The fisherman's daughter, who becomes pregnant, is enacted by Ingrid Bergman. [She is] superb! She is an obvious asset to Swedish film. Her face, which has sometimes been photographed in a somewhat sentimental mood, is pleasant to study. Her acting in this sensitive film is well-balanced and tender. . . . She is gracious and true.

In *Dagens Nyheter* (Swedish):

Ingrid Bergman is more than acceptable in the feminine lead. One did believe in her tenderness and faithfulness.

In *Stockholms-Tidningen* (Swedish):

The old ones act best. Ingrid Bergman is almost better.

Strom) and his overwhelming desire for her leads to a sin of lust. Overcome by remorse, he runs out into the stormy night, calls upon God, and is hit by a bolt of lightning. He becomes an amnesiac and is sent away to be cured. Karin finds herself pregnant, but bears her child in proud silence and refuses to divulge the name of the father. When the minister has been cured, and returns to the village and his pastorate, he is conscience-stricken by the sight of mother and child and publicly confesses his sin to the entire village after a sermon, in which he says that in him God had a poor servant. He abandons his ministry, becomes a farmer, and the turbulence and guilt in his heart are exorcised.

REVIEWS

In Social-Demokraten (Swedish):

Ingrid Bergman [is] the heroine. Her qualifications so far rest mostly in her striking, plethoric type, which shows promise for the future.

Swedenhielms

Svenskfilmindustri, 1935

CAST

Gosta Ekman, Karin Swanstrom, Bjorn Berglund, Hakan Westergren, Tutta Rolf, Ingrid Bergman, Sigurd Wallen, Nils Ericsson, Adele Soderblom, Mona Geijer-Falkner, Hjalmar Peters.

CREDITS

Produced by AB Svenskfilmindustri. Directed by Gustaf Molander. Screenplay by Stina Bergman from the play by Hjalmar Bergman. Photo-

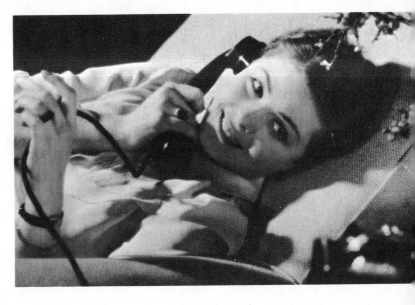

graphed by Ake Dahlquist. Music by Helge Lindberg. Premiere, Roda Kvarn, August 4, 1935. Shown at Venice Film Festival, 1935. Length, 2518 meters. (American premiere, Cinema de Paris, New York, September 1935.)

THE STORY

Rolf Swedenhielm *(Gosta Ekman)* is a Swedish scientist who lacks financial practicality and loses himself in his research work. He has left the raising of his now-grown children, Rolf Jr., Bo and Julia *(Bjorn Berglund, Hakan Westergren* and *Tutta Rolf)* largely to his steady-minded and practical sister-in-law and housekeeper, Marta Boman *(Karin Swanstrom)*. Bo is engaged to Astrid *(Ingrid Bergman)* a wealthy girl, but since his own financial prospects are dim, Bo hesitates out of pride to marry her and accept her financial aid, though Astrid is perfectly willing to go along with such an arrangement. Astrid appeals to Swedenhielm on the matter, but he declares that his son's self-respect is important and he must do as he sees fit. This decision irritates Astrid, who thinks the entire family as impractical as Marta does. Swedenhielm learns from his foster-brother, Eriksson *(Sigurd Wallen)*, a usurer, that Eriksson has bought up promissory notes on which Swedenhielm's signature has been forged—by Bo, allegedly. Eriksson has an ancient grudge against Swedenhielm, and enjoys the opportunity to embarrass the scientist. Swedenhielm is so shocked and grieved that when he is offered the Nobel Prize he feels that he should refuse it, because his son is about to be

With Hakan Westergren

exposed for forgery. When confronted with the notes, Bo's reaction is equivocal. It develops that he was trying to protect his brother, Rolf Jr., whom he suspected of the forgery. At this point Marta comes forward and declares that she signed the notes in Swedenhielm's name because it was the only way she could obtain funds to run the household, what with all the financial impracticality to which the entire family was given. A happy ending is presaged, a relieved Swedenhielm goes back to his scientific ruminations, and the rest of the family goes on as usual, under the watchful eye of the long-suffering and long-exasperated Marta.

REVIEWS

In Dagens Nyheter (Swedish, 1935):

An elegant, charming film, blessedly free from stereotyped characterizations or romanticism. Received with hearty applause.

In Svenska Dagbladet (Swedish, 1935):

Swedish film production has, for the first time in many years, reached not only international standards but even high international standards.

With Gosta Ekman and director
Gustaf Molander

In Stockholms-Tidningen (Swedish, 1935):

It is the emotion that carries you away. A river of warm emotion runs through the entire film. It is a beautiful emotion, it is powerful and it shows dignity. You might call it a Swedish emotion. We have seen a great many well-made movies, we have been subjected to those that are polished on the surface and elegant. Here, though, comes a film which is technically perfect and at the same time pregnantly rich as far as its contents go. It is also carried along by an inspired sensitivity.

In Berlin am Mittag (German):

This Swedish sound film has had an enormous success. There are three outstanding qualities of the performance to thank: the intellectual content, the marvelous photography and the extraordinary characterizations. Stina Bergman's screenplay has accurately followed Hjalmar Bergman's play. . . . Gustaf Molander's film, photographed by Ake Dahlquist, affectionately follows the curve of the comedy. . . . Ingrid Bergman [is] feelingful.

48

With Victor Seastrom

Valborgsmassoafton

(Walpurgis Night)

Svenskfilmindustri, 1935

CAST

Lars Hanson, Karin Carlsson, Victor Seastrom, Ingrid Bergman, Erik Berglund, Sture Lagerwall, Georg Rydeberg, Georg Blickingberg, Rickard Lund, Stig Jarrel, Marie-Louise Sorbon, Gabriel Alw, Carl-Gunnar Wingard, Aino Taube, Torsten Hillberg, Anders Hendriksson, Torsten Winge, Greta Berthels, Ake Uppstrom, Linnea Hillberg, Ivar Kage, Lill-Acke, Olaf Widgren, Hjalmar Peters, Pecka Hagman, Harry Hednoff.

CREDITS

Produced by AB Svenskfilmindustri. Directed by Gustaf Edgren. Screenplay by Oscar Rydquist and Gustaf Edgren from their original story. Photographed by Martin Bodin. Premiere at Spegeln Theatre, Stockholm, October 23, 1935. Shown at the 48th Street Theatre, New York, January 1941. Length, 2229 meters.

THE STORY

Lena Bergstrom *(Ingrid Bergman)*, secretary to her married employer, Johan Borg *(Lars Hanson)*, is the daughter of crusading newspaper editor Fredrik Bergstrom *(Victor Seastrom)*, who publicly deplores Sweden's falling birthrate and the increasing disinterest in children. Lena is desperately in love with Johan, who is burdened with a cold and selfish wife, Clary *(Karin Carlsson)*, who denies Johan his marital rights because she fears childbirth and what she thinks will be its effect on her appearance. Clary, despite her precautions, finds herself pregnant and visits an abortionist. Later she is blackmailed by an underworld character who has stolen the record of her operation from the abortionist's office. In struggling with the blackmailer for the record, Clary shoots and kills him. Later she commits suicide. The case develops into a front-page scandal in Fredrik's newspaper. Later Johan, shocked, joins the Foreign Legion. Eventually he returns to Sweden and takes up a life with the ever-loving and loyal Lena, which includes not only marriage but the babies Clary denied him.

REVIEWS

Nils Edgren in Social-Demokraten (Swedish):

A film of the kind which justifies the talk about a new great era for the Swedish film. The opening night audience greeted it with resounding benevolence and there was applause more than once.

With Lars Hanson

Dorothy Masters in the New York Daily News (1941):

[The film] is a fruit from the censor's forbidden tree, and as such, liable for ensuing aches and pains for two reasons. Those who partake of its full flavor will suffer through all the tragic ramifications of a powerful drama; some who don't partake will be pained that such a subject as abortion should ever have found its way into celluloid. In any event, the film from Sweden has

With Lars Hanson

In Svenska Dagbladet (Swedish):

One of the best films of the Swedish sound film epoch. I do not think there has ever been better acting in a Swedish film. It was received with warm applause, which was well-deserved.

In Dagens Nyheter (Swedish):

A Swedish film with strong, true, warm feelings. And a Swedish film which at the same time carries a message, while it is also dramatically entertaining. [The film] does honor not only to its originators, it does so also to Swedish films as a whole.

an emotional quality that cannot be gainsaid, a cast of able, sincere players, and a moral of great weight. . . . Victor Seastrom gives a memorable performance. . . . Ingrid Bergman gives an able portrayal as the daughter. (Rated 3 Stars on *Daily News* chart.)

Irene Thirer in the New York Post (1941):

[*Walpurgis Night*] presents lovely Ingrid Bergman in a problem picture which was made some six years ago and bears the brunt of abrupt editing, on account of a censorable subject which has kept it from release here up to now. . . . Yet outside of this situation (abortion) the picture is straightaway melodrama. (Rated Fair on New York *Post*'s Poor-Fair-Good-Excellent movie barometer.)

With Lars Hanson

With Lars Hanson

Pa Solsidan

(On the Sunny Side)

Svenskfilmindustri, 1936.

CAST

Lars Hanson, Ingrid Bergman, Karin Swanstrom, Edvin Adolphson, Einar Axelson, Marianne Lofgren, Carl Browallius, Bullen Berglund, Eddie Figge, Olga Andersson, Viktor Andersson, Eric Gustafsson.

CREDITS

Produced by Aktiebolaget Wivefilm. Directed by Gustaf Molander. Screenplay by Oscar Hemberg and Gosta Stevens from the play by Helge Krog. Photographed by Ake Dahlquist. Music arranged by Eric Bengtsson. Premiere, Spegeln Theatre, Stockholm, March 2, 1936. American Premiere, Cinema de Paris Theatre, New York, August 1936. Length, 2620 meters.

THE STORY

Eva Bergh (*Ingrid Bergman*), a well-born orphan, works as a bank clerk. Her father was an artist, and she has inherited some of his bohemian ways, but not his talent. During a birthday party tendered her by some of her bohemian friends, she is accosted by a young writer, Joakim Brink (*Edvin Adolphson*), and while she is mildly attracted to him, his seduction attempts fail. She then becomes involved with a wealthy country gentleman, Harold Ribe (*Lars Hanson*), whose shy and conservative ways win her admiration and respect, and, finally, her love. Harold and Eva marry, but Harold, comparing their quiet life at his country estate, Sunnyside, with the gay and exciting existence Eva led in the city, worries lest she find her current existence slow and tedious. He invites some of her city friends to their estate, and complications ensue when

With Edvin Adolphson

51

Harold becomes upset and fearful that Eva still finds Joakim attractive. Meanwhile Joakim has fallen in love with Harold's sister, Kajsa *(Marianne Lofgren)*. The misunderstandings are eventually straightened out, and Eva and Harold find permanent security in their happiness together.

REVIEWS

In Nya Dagligt Allehanda (Swedish):

Ingrid Bergman's great break-through. . . . She not only supported her skilled partner (Lars Hanson) superbly; she sometimes was his absolute equal.

In Social-Demokraten (Swedish):

Ingrid Bergman is blindingly beautiful and acts with strong inspiration. She handles her every line with perfection.

In Svenska Dagbladet (Swedish):

Ingrid Bergman has matured as an actress and a woman. One simply must give up before her beauty and talent. [Miss Bergman] is not only beautiful; she has the ability to express, mimewise, the emotions she has in her.

Shan. in Variety:

With an agile cast and a sprinkling of native wit, although deficient in action and somewhat incohesive, this Swedish picture should prove a best-seller in the Svensk nabes. It has moments of nice photography. Quite a chatty piece, the plot is mostly inconsequential. One of the better characterizations in the play is that of *(Ingrid*

With Einar Axelson

Bergman) the lead. She is pretty and capable, rating a Hollywood berth. Edvin Adolphson and Einar Axelson are to be commended also. Both prove their aptitude for serio-comedy roles.

H.T.S. in The New York Times:

The natural charm of Ingrid Bergman, the young Stockholm actress whose star has risen so rapidly in the Scandinavian film firmament, makes it worthwhile visiting the Cinema de París to see *Pa Solsidan (On the Sunny Side)*, the first Swedish importation of the new season. . . . While the acting of all the principals is excellent, Miss Bergman dominates the field throughout. The comedy is in good taste but the film is photographed theatre rather than a movie.

With Edvin Adolphson and Lars Hanson

Intermezzo (Swedish Version)

Svenskfilmindustri, 1936

CAST

Gosta Ekman, Inga Tidblad, Hans Ekman, Britt Hagman, Erik Berglund, Ingrid Bergman, Hugo Bjorne, Emma Meissner, Anders Henrikson, Millan Bolander, George Fant, Folke Helleberg, Margit Orth, Carl Strom.

CREDITS

Produced by AB Svenskfilmindustri. Directed by Gustaf Molander. Screenplay by Gustaf Molander and Gosta Stevens from an original story by Mr. Molander. Photographed by Ake Dahlquist. Music by Heinz Provost.* Leitmotif "Intermezzo" composed by Mr. Provost. Premiere, Roda Kvarn, Stockholm, November 16, 1936. Length, 2523 meters. Shown in New York at the Cinema de Paris, December 1937. Running time, 88 minutes. English subtitles.

* Violin: Charles Barkel
Piano: Stina Sundell

NOTE

The film was remade in Hollywood by David O. Selznick in 1939 with Miss Bergman repeating the role of Anita Hoffman and Leslie Howard as Holger Brandt.

THE STORY

World-famous violinist Holger Brandt (*Gosta Ekman*) returns to Sweden from a tour. He is greeted by his wife, Margit (*Inga Tidblad*), and his children, Ake (*Hans Ekman*) and Ann-Marie (*Britt Hagman*). Later he meets Anita Hoffman (*Ingrid Bergman*), pupil of Holger's accompanist, Thomas Stenborg (*Hugo Bjorne*). Anita is Ann-Marie's piano teacher, and Holger is electrified by Anita's own excellent playing at a party, and he accompanies her on his violin. Later Holger and Anita meet accidentally and go for refresh-

With Gosta Ekman

ments at a restaurant. Gradually they drift into a passionate love affair. They find themselves too weak to resist their love, despite the inevitable unhappiness they know they will cause others, and go away together on a tour of Europe, with Anita serving as Holger's accompanist. For a time they are happy, but Anita realizes that Holger misses Ann-Marie and his former secure life and though she loves him as much as ever, leaves him to resume her career elsewhere.

With Gosta Ekman

54

Gosta Ekman

Holger returns at last to Sweden, and is reunited with the patiently waiting Margit after his child, Ann-Marie, is injured while running across the street to be reunited with him. Ann-Marie's recovery is indicated, along with future happiness for Holger and Margit. But he knows that Anita will always live in a small corner of his heart.

REVIEWS

In Aftonbladet (Swedish):

Stevens here proves himself an accomplished script-writer. . . . a warmly human and true conflict is the basis of his firmly-shaped, original manuscript, which has been transposed with the same unfailing elegance and good taste as always. Gustaf Molander has handled this task. . . . It is, however, not only the beautiful framework, the superb music and the interesting conflict which captures one in this film but to a much higher degree the excellent acting.

In Ny Tid (Swedish):

Ingrid Bergman adds a new victory to her past ones via this film. The strongest Swedish movie that has come along in a very long time.

In Arbetaren (Swedish):

Apart from the special Swedish acting tempo, [*Intermezzo* is] a beautiful film which can be seen with rewarding results. It is a plus in Swedish film production in the year 1936.

In Svenska Dagbladet (Swedish):

It does honor both to Svenskfilmindustri and the Swedish film in general. There was no applause at the end of the early opening night show, but that was because the audience was enraptured. By a Swedish film yet!

H.T.S. in The New York Times (1937):

Charming Miss Bergman confirms the good opinions she won at home and abroad in former pictures.

R.W.D. in the New York Herald Tribune (1937):

The biggest compliment that can be paid the entire cast is that they are as natural as people we might pass in the streets at any time, at any place. . . . Molander has directed the film superbly and the photography is letter perfect.

In Variety (1937):

Intermezzo takes its place among the finest foreign pictures to be shown on American soil this year. It is poignant, full of pathos, and above all, has shown, in Ingrid Bergman, a talented, beautiful actress. Miss Bergman's star is destined for Hollywood.

Dollar

Svenskfilmindustri, 1938

CAST

Georg Rydeberg, Ingrid Bergman, Kotti Chave, Tutta Rolf, Hakan Westergren, Birgit Tengroth, Elsa Burnett, Edvin Adolphson, Gosta Cederlund, Eric Rosen, Carl Strom, Alex Hogel, Millan Bolander, David Eriksson, Erland Colliander, Nils Dahlgren, Gustav Lagerberg, Richard Lindstrom, E. Dethorey, Dickson, Aina Elkman, Hester Harvey, Helge Kihlberg, Allan Linder.

CREDITS

Produced by AB Svenskfilmindustri. Directed by Gustaf Molander, Screenplay by Stina Bergman and Gustaf Molander from the comedy by Hjalmar Bergman. Photographed by Ake Dahlquist. Music arranged by Eric Bengtsson. Premiere, China Theatre, May 9, 1938.

THE STORY

Julia Balzar *(Ingrid Bergman),* a beautiful actress, is married to sturdy and dependable businessman, Kurt Balzar *(Georg Rydeberg).* Katja *(Birgit Tengroth),* a simple, uncomplicated type, is married to a rich man of the world, Ludwig von Battwyhl *(Hakan Westergren).* A third couple are the nervous, high-strung Sussi *(Tutta Rolf)* and her roguish husband, Lt. Louis Brenner *(Kotti Chave),* who constantly loses money at card games. All suspect his or her mate of having affairs with someone else's spouse. Julia feels that Kurt neglects her for his business, SVEA, Inc. Kurt, on the other hand, feels that his wife is infatuated with the handsome rakish Louis.

One night Louis ruins himself in a card game, and Julia, anxious to save him, sells her shares in SVEA to pay his gambling debts. This causes a stock market panic and Kurt is threatened with bankruptcy. Julia says nothing, but Ludwig buys her shares before the market is drastically affected and promises Julia that he will not tell her husband.

A wealthy American relative of Kurt, Mary Johnstone *(Elsa Burnett),* announces her arrival

With Hakan Westergren

With Kotti Chave

at a ski lodge to which all the couples have repaired. Sussi meanwhile suspects that Julia has paid her husband's debts and she fears that they are having an affair. Distraught, she loses her way to the lodge and the American rescues her. Sussi's experience in the storm and her jealousy of Julia affect her psychosomatically and she cannot walk. Mary registers her disgust with the couples' extra-marital love affairs, reveals that Julia sold the SVEA stock and makes Sussi so angry with her accusations and revelations that she finds she can walk again. Meanwhile Mary has fallen in love with the hotel clerk, Dr. Johnson *(Edvin Adolphson)*. Somehow the various couples adjust their differences, Mary and Dr. Johnson marry and now there are *four* happy marrieds.

REVIEWS

In Dagens Nyheter (Swedish):

It is not every day that one is permitted to watch a Swedish comedy as spirited and charming as *Dollar*. It has been staged according to the best rules of the art and its acting conveys a glad and joyous note.

In Svenska Dagbladet (Swedish):

Ingrid Bergman's feline appearance as an industrial tycoon's wife overshadows them all...

partly because of her dominant role, far removed from the ones she usually plays; also, however, owing to [her] superb comedy timing and her lustrous appearance.

In Stockholms-Tidningen (Swedish):

A parade show of what Swedish directors, photographers, actors and technicians can accomplish today.

With Tutta Rolf

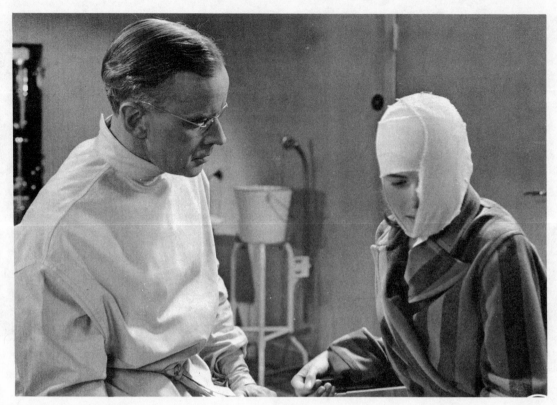

En Kvinnas Ansíkte

(A Woman's Face)

Svenskfilmindustri, 1938

CAST

Ingrid Bergman, Anders Henrikson, Erik Berglund, Magnus Kesster, Gosta Cederlund, Georg Rydeberg, Tore Svennberg, Goran Bernhard, Gunnar Sjoberg, Hilda Borgstrom, John Ericsson, Karin Carlsson-Kavli, Sigurd Wallen, Bror Bugler.

CREDITS

Produced by AB Svenskfilmindustri. Directed by Gustaf Molander. Screenplay by Gosta Stevens from the play Il Etait Une Fois by Francois de Croisset. Photographed by Ake Dahlquist. Length, 2852 meters. Premiere, Roda Kvarn, Stockholm, October 31, 1938. Shown in New York at the 48th Street Theatre in September 1939. English dialogue. Running time, 100 minutes.

NOTE

The film was later remade by Metro-Goldwyn-Mayer in Hollywood in 1941 and starred Joan Crawford in Miss Bergman's role of Anna Holm.

THE STORY

Anna Holm *(Ingrid Bergman)* in childhood sustained a hideous facial scar which has marred her adult life. Embittered and emotionally deadened, she has taken to leading a ring of blackmailers. She encounters Torsten Barring *(Georg Rydeberg)*, a scheming aristocrat who senses her loneliness and emotional vulnerability and wins her over, with the thought that she may be useful to him in the future. While attempting to blackmail Fru Wegert *(Karin Carlsson-Kavli)*, the wife of Dr. Wegert *(Anders Henrikson)*, a noted

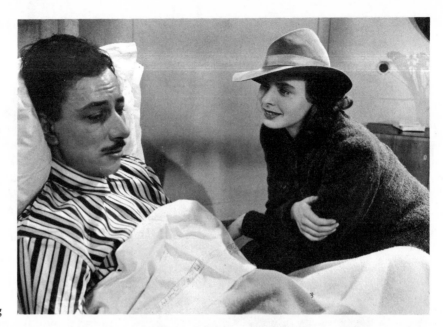

With Gunnar Sjoberg

plastic surgeon, she accidentally encounters the doctor, who, noting her pitifully scarred features, suggests a complicated and painful operation, which Anna undergoes. The operation is successful and she goes to Barring hoping that now there will be a possibility of a life for them together, but he has other ideas. He proposes to use her in an evil scheme to murder his nephew, Lars-Erik *(Goran Bernhard),* so that Torsten will be the sole heir to the fortune of his father, Consul Magnus Barring *(Tore Svennberg).* Anna, though somewhat repelled, is still in love with Torsten, and takes the position of governess in the Barring household to carry out their scheme. But the restoration of her now-beautiful features has also resulted in a rejuvenation and ennoblement of her spirit, and she refuses to carry out the planned murder of young Lars-Erik. An enraged Torsten attempts to kill the boy during a wild sleighride across the wintry Swedish countryside, but is shot by Anna, who has followed with Wegert in another sleigh. Anna is placed on trial for murder, but a successful plea of justifiable homicide is eventually indicated.

With Goran Bernhard

With Georg Rydeberg

REVIEWS

Herbert Cohn in The Brooklyn Daily Eagle (1939):

Ingrid Bergman . . . demonstrates as Anna that she is an effective actress as well as a charming one.

In Variety (1939):

[Miss Bergman] is superb in the general display of thespian pyrotechnics. In the lead role, she magnificently portrays the soul-seared girl whom fate, through an accident, decreed to suffer the ignominy of scarred tissue and bitterness. . . . Gustaf Molander, Sweden's ace director, who worked with Miss Bergman in *Intermezzo* two years ago, with the late Gosta Ekman as co-star, has done an exceptionally good job of pacing the film well.

Dorothy Masters in The New York Daily News (1939):

Ingrid Bergman, whose brilliant performance in *Intermezzo* resulted in her importation to Hollywood for an American version of that Swedish film, opens the season at the 48th Street Theatre with another exceptional drama. *En Kvinnas Ansikte*, starkly presented and unusual in theme, is a triumph not only for Miss Bergman but for the cast, the technicians and the Swedish cinema as well. . . . The film is too good to be limited to Swedish audiences.

In The New York World-Telegram (1939):

Ingrid Bergman is another Garbo . . . as good as Garbo in her earliest efforts. Given a part that tugs at every emotion, she reveals ever-increasing possibilities. Gustaf Molander has contributed several unforgettable moments in the direction. And the supporting players, notably Anders Henrikson and Hilda Borgstrom, are superb. A film which, in a word, is adult.

"Robin Hood"* in Stockholms-Tidningen (Swedish):

No Swedish film has in a long time been so perfect and internationally first-class in its technique. A script that, for once, is full of suspense to the very end and joins the characterization with a criminal intrigue.

Ellen Lilliedahl** in Svenska Dagbladet (Swedish):

[The film] lacks muscle, dynamic force, artistic truth. Once again artistic strength has been wasted upon a puny task, upon a hack script which barely rises above the level of the yellow press.

* "Robin Hood" was the pen-name of B. Idestam-Almquist, a well-known Swedish critic of the period.

** Ellen Lilliedahl was known as the dissenter of the Swedish film critics. She usually did not like what the majority of her colleagues admired, and she was regarded in Swedish film circles as honest and trenchant—or destructive and cantankerous, depending on who was giving an opinion.

En Enda Natt

(Only One Night)

Svenskfilmindustri, 1939

CAST

Ingrid Bergman, Edvin Adolphson, Aino Taube, Olof Sandborg, Erik "Bullen" Berglund, Marianne Lofgren, Magnus Kesster, Sophus Dahl, Ragna Breda, John Eklof, Tor Borong, Viktor "Kulorten" Andersson, Ka Nerell, Folke Helleberg, Nila Nordstahl.

CREDITS

Produced by AB Svenskfilmindustri. Directed by Gustaf Molander. Screenplay by Gosta Stevens from the story "En Eneste Natt" by Harald Tandrup. Assistant director: Hugo Bolander. Premiere, Roda Kvarn, Stockholm, March 13, 1939. Shown in New York at the 48th Street Theatre, December 1942. English subtitles. Length, 2477 meters. (American release by Scandia Films. Running time, 89 minutes.)

THE STORY

Valdemar Moreaux (Edvin Adolphson), a handsome young circus attendant, is recognized as the illegitimate son of a wealthy old aristocrat, Magnus von Brede (Olof Sandborg), and is invited by his father to assume his rightful heritage. Valdemar has been living with the circus proprietress, Helga Martensson (Aino Taube), and is reluctant to leave her. He finds it difficult to accustom himself to a life of wealth and refinement, and when von Brede tries to foster a romantic attachment between Valdemar and von Brede's beautiful young ward, Eva (Ingrid Bergman), with an idea of marrying them off to each other, Valdemar and Eva demonstrate minds of their own and resist the scheme. However, Valdemar gradually falls in love with the beautiful and ladylike Eva. Ill at ease in his posh sur-

With Edvin Adolphson

With Edvin Adolphson

roundings, crude in his approaches, Valdemar gets drunk and tries to force his attentions on Eva, who rejects him. Fully realizing that Eva does not requite his feelings, he returns to the circus and marries Helga, who, he is now aware, is in all respects the right woman for him.

REVIEWS

Archer Winsten in the New York Post (1942):

En Enda Natt is a surprisingly interesting picture. Miss Bergman proves that she had very little to learn when she came to this country. Her ability in portraying gradations of the love emotion now being demonstrated in *Casablanca* at the Hollywood Theatre is no less evident in her older Swedish film. On one occasion she even sings a song in English, thus indicating that the language itself was not beyond her early powers. When you think of going to see *En Enda Natt* do not consider it an antique and amusing slant on an actress now on her way to the top. Bergman in this picture is an artist in good control of her considerable powers. By the same token, the picture itself is no wooden antique.... Whoever in Hollywood discovered Miss Bergman doesn't deserve much credit. No one could have missed her talent.

T.M.P. in The New York Times (1942):

Aside from affording an opportunity to observe Ingrid Bergman in one of her last pre-

With Olof Sandborg

Hollywood pictures, *En Enda Natt,* the new Swedish importation at the 48th Street Theatre, is in its own right an engrossing drama of conflicting human emotions. To audiences accustomed to film drama woven around romantic and psychological patterns within the confines of the Hays Office purity code, *En Enda Natt* no doubt will seem surprisingly adult, if not slightly risque in two sequences. In fact the theme as a whole (illegitimacy and extra-marital sex) is one that Hollywood seldom deals with, and when it does, approaches the subject with such skittishness that the results are generally disappointing, to say the least. . . . As the principals, Miss Bergman and Edvin Adolphson are excellent and lesser roles are admirably played by Olof Sandborg and Aino Taube. . . . Though the middle portion of the picture tends to drag, *En Enda Natt* is nevertheless an absorbing drama.

In Arbetaren (Swedish):

[The film] contains fairly probing psychology and superb detail studies. Gustaf Molander's direction has brought about a good result, and all in all, it can be said that Swedish film has truly attained a splendid end effect.

In Social-Demokraten (Swedish):

As a type, Ingrid Bergman, playing the upper-class girl, represents a rare kind of woman with erotic complexes. Miss Bergman handles the role with great finesse.

With Sabine Peters, Ursula Herking, Carsta Lock.

Die Vier Gesellen

(The Four Companions)

UFA, 1938

CAST

Ingrid Bergman, Sabine Peters, Ursula Herking, Carsta Lock, Hans Sohnker, Leo Slezak, Heinz Weizel, Willi Rose, Erich Ponto, Karl Haubenreiber, Wilhelm P. Kruger, Lotte Braun, Hugo Froelich, Rudolf Klicks, Max Rosenhauer, Ernst G. Schiffner, Hans Jurgen Weidlich.

CREDITS

Produced by UFA in Germany in 1938. Sole rights to Svenskfilmindustri. Directed by Carl Froelich. Screenplay by Jochen Huth from his play. Length, 2648 meters.

THE STORY

Four girls who have become good companions while attending a school of industrial art decide to form an advertising agency after graduation.

The girls are Marianne (Ingrid Bergman); Lotte (Carsta Lock); Kathe (Sabine Peters); and Franziska (Ursula Herking). At the graduation party their young teacher, Stefan Kohlund (Hans Sohnker), proposes marriage to Marianne, but though she is somewhat attracted to him, she turns him down, in order to prove that she can make her own way. Later the girls start the agency, which they title "Die Vier Gesellen" ("The Four Apprentices"), and after overcoming initial difficulties, begin to achieve success. Part of their success depends on their publicity campaign for a company in which Kohlund is now employed. Kohlund does not know that Marianne and her friends are heading the agency. He and Marianne meet again, but she continues to resist his marriage proposal. Life, meanwhile, has visited

With Heinz Welzel

varying fortunes on the other girls. One decides to forsake a career for marriage and goes happily off with her new husband. Another finds that the price of pre-marital sex is embarrassment and hurt and she marries to give her baby a name and a home. A third decides to abandon commerce for serious painting. Now that the other girls have deserted "The Four Apprentices" for varying reasons, Marianne decides that working on her own is no fun and at last accepts Stefan's proposal.

REVIEWS

In Aftonbladet (Swedish):

Opens all right, but that is soon over. In the long run, it becomes chatty and lacking in interest.

In Social-Demokraten (Swedish):

Self-assured, elegant and fresh as a daisy, Ingrid Bergman creates full illusion in her part. The acting in the quartet, however, is really done by a dark, ugly girl whose name is Ursula Herking and who plays the great talent among the four.

With Hans Sohnker

In Svenska Dagbladet (Swedish):

The plot does not lack its good points, amusing scenes and lines as well as bits of bitterly sad sentiment. As a whole, though, it is too long-winded and thin to really generate any interest.

In Folkets Dagblad (Swedish):

It does not even help that Ingrid Bergman looks at the audience with beautiful, sad eyes.

Juninatten

(A Night in June)

Svenskfilmindustri, 1940

CAST

Ingrid Bergman, Marianne Lofgren, Lill-Tollie Zellman, Marianne Aminoff, Olof Widgren, Gunnar Sjoberg, Gabriel Alw, Olof Winnerstrand, Sigurd Wallen, Hasse Ekman, Maritta Marke, Gudrun Brost, John Botvid, Karin Swanstrom, Carl Strom, Mimi Pollak, Charlie Paterson, Ernst Brunman, Alf Kjellin, Karin Nordgren, Mona Geijer-Falkner, David Eriksson, Douglas Hage, Carl Deurell, Sven-Goran Alw, Richard Lund, Nils Jacobsson, Sol-Britt Agerup, Kerstin Ekwall, Britta Larsson, Viran Rydkvist, Erik Forslund.

CREDITS

Produced by AB Svenskfilmindustri. Directed by Per Lindberg. Screenplay by Ragnar Hylten-Cavallius from a story by Tora Nordstrom-Bonnier. Photographed by Ake Dahlquist. Film editor, Oscar Rosander. Music by Jules Sylvain. Co-arranger, Gunnar Johansson. Assistant director, Hugo Bolander. Premiere, Roda Kvarn, Stockholm, March 4, 1940. Length, 2440 meters.

THE STORY

Kerstin Nordback (Ingrid Bergman), a sensitive and cultured young girl without family or friends, works at an apothecary in a small Swedish town. She lives in a boardinghouse, where her landlady spies on her constantly to learn if she is associating with men. The manners and mores of the little town are stultifying to Kerstin's beauty-loving spirit. At the public library she meets a sailor, Nils Asklund (Gunnar Sjoberg),

With Gunnar Sjoberg

who is likewise lonely and rootless and who tells her about the great world outside. Attracted to him and basking in the human warmth he offers, she gives herself to him.

They begin an affair but the difference in their background and life-aims soon becomes apparent, and when Kerstin threatens to leave Nils, he draws out a gun and threatens suicide. The gun goes off and Kerstin is hit near her heart. Careful surgery aids her in a recovery.

At the subsequent trial Nils establishes that he actually meant to kill himself, and he receives a relatively light sentence, a few years in prison, due partly to Kerstin's compassionate plea in his behalf. But the affair has created a scandal in the stuffy little town, especially after a Stockholm

With Olaf Widgren

paper heavily publicizes it, and Doctor Berggren *(Carl Strom)* aids Kerstin in obtaining a position with an apothecary in Stockholm. There she is asked to change her name, and so she becomes Sara Nordana. In Stockholm she meets Stefan Von Bremen *(Olof Widgren)*, a young man who is well suited to her culturally and spiritually, and they find happiness together.

REVIEWS

Mac Lindahl in Oresunds-Posten (Swedish):

Juninatten above all wants to be honest, absolutely frank as a picture of a piece of living Stockholm. This ambition has been met in a surprising manner. Ingrid Bergman, with her portrayal of Sara Nordana, establishes herself as an actress belonging to the world elite.

In Boras Nyheter (Swedish):

Per Lindberg's direction and Ingrid Bergman's acting in this film do not suffer from a comparison with good foreign films. The photography is some of the best ever seen in a Swedish film.

In Stockholms Lans Tidning (Swedish):

Ingrid Bergman shows, in *Juninatten*, that Swedish film art can create works of art that are of the highest class. The film is, above all, a triumph for her.

In Arbetaren (Swedish):

Ingrid Bergman lived her part. It was obvious that she had fully understood her assignment.

With Marianne Aminoff

International Fame

Intermezzo (A Love Story)

Selznick International-United Artists, 1939

CAST

Leslie Howard, Ingrid Bergman, Edna Best, John Halliday, Cecil Kellaway, Enid Bennett, Ann Todd, Douglas Scott, Eleanor Wesselhoeft, Moira Flynn.

CREDITS

A Selznick-International Production for United Artists Release. Produced by David O. Selznick. Directed by Gregory Ratoff. Associate producer, Leslie Howard. Screenplay by George O'Neil based on the original Swedish screen scenario, Intermezzo by Gosta Stevens and Gustaf Molander. Musical director, Lou Forbes. Cameraman: Gregg Toland. Film editors: Hal C. Kern and Francis D. Lyon. Running time, 70 minutes.

THE STORY

Holger Brandt (Leslie Howard), a celebrated Swedish violinist, returns from a triumphal tour abroad with his accompanist, Thomas Stenborg (John Halliday), to his wife Margit (Edna Best) and his children, Ann Marie (Ann Todd) and Eric (Douglas Scott). During a party at his home he meets Anita Hoffman (Ingrid Bergman), a pupil of Stenborg's and Ann Marie's piano teacher. Holger is enthralled by Anita's sensitively dynamic playing, which he accompanies on his violin. Holger meets Anita by accident some days later at a concert, and they go to a cafe and talk. They are drawn to each other and the initially casual meetings grow in intensity unfil they discover they are deeply in love. They try to break apart, but Holger eventually tells Margit that he wants his freedom, and he and Anita go abroad, with Anita as his accompanist. Their love flourishes idyllically for a time, but Anita realizes

increasingly that he misses his children and former life.

At great emotional cost to herself, she leaves him for a concert career after a worried and compassionate Thomas, while visiting them, asks her: "I wonder if happiness was ever built on the unhappiness of others?" Holger returns home to Sweden. Ann Marie, running across a street from school to greet her father, is seriously injured, and later a grief-stricken Holger, awaiting her recovery, wins back his hurt and lonely young son and is welcomed back with gladness by the estranged wife who has never ceased to love and wait for him.

With Leslie Howard

With Leslie Howard

REVIEWS

Frank S. Nugent in The New York Times:

Sweden's Ingrid Bergman is so lovely a person and so gracious an actress that we are rather glad David Selznick selected the quiet *Intermezzo—A Love Story* for her Hollywood debut instead of some more bravura drama, which, while it might not have overwhelmed its star, might have overwhelmed us, and made us less conscious of the freshness, the simplicity and the natural dignity that are Miss Bergman's pleasant gifts to our screen. . . . She is beautiful and not at all pretty.

Her acting is surprisingly mature, yet singularly free from the stylistic traits—the mannerisms, postures, precise inflections—that become the stock in trade of the matured actress. Our impression of her Anita, who is pallid one moment, vivacious the next, yet always consistent, is that of a lamp whose wick burns bright or dull, but always burns. There is that incandescence about Miss Bergman, that spiritual spark which makes us believe that Selznick has found another great lady of the screen. . . . [The picture] is not exactly a dramatic thunderbolt, nothing the glamour-conscious will be inflamed about. But we

With Leslie Howard

found it a mature, an eloquent, and a sensitive film and we recommend it to you.

Howard Barnes in the New York Herald Tribune:

In remaking the Swedish film, *Intermezzo*, as the Hollywood film, *Intermezzo—A Love Story*, David O. Selznick was exceedingly smart in sticking to the lovely leading lady of the original. Ingrid Bergman is her name, and her presence [in the film] is its chief distinction. She has natural assurance and dignity as well as an exciting talent. . . . Using scarcely any makeup, but playing with mobile intensity, she creates the character so vividly and credibly that it becomes the core of what narrative there is. . . . Although new to Hollywood, Miss Bergman has had more than a little acting experience abroad, and it stands her in good stead. To my mind she is the most gifted and attractive recruit that the studios have enlisted from abroad for many moons.

David Hanna in Film Bulletin:

Tall, beautiful, emotional and a superb actress, Ingrid Bergman is a new addition to the American screen worth raving about. Her performance in this is exquisite, beautifully shaded, exerting a vivid dramatic effect on the spectator.

Archer Winsten in the New York Post:

[Miss Bergman] seems to be a healthy, well-set-up young lady, good-looking, able to smile very charmingly, and possessed of rare acting ability.

In Variety:

[Ingrid Bergman] is beautiful, talented, and convincing, providing an arresting performance and a warm personality that introduces a new stellar asset to Hollywood. She has charm, sincerity, and an infectious vivaciousness that will serve her well in both drama and comedy.

In the New York Journal-American:

Miss Bergman plays with persuasive charm and conviction.

Wanda Hale in the New York Daily News:

Quietly stirring as the plaintive tones of a violin . . . told beautifully and simply. [Ingrid Bergman] is the finest thing that has come to Hollywood from anywhere in many a day. It is extremely unfair to call her a second Garbo, just because she hails from Sweden. She has a combination of rare beauty, freshness, vitality and ability that is as uncommon as a century plant in bloom.

Adam Had Four Sons

Columbia, 1941

CAST

Ingrid Bergman, Warner Baxter, Susan Hayward, Fay Wray, Richard Denning, Johnny Downs, Robert Shaw, Charles Lind, Helen Westley, June Lockhart, Pete Sosso, Gilbert Emery, Renie Riano, Clarence Muse, Billy Ray, Steven Muller, Wallace Chadwell, Bobby Walberg.

CREDITS

Produced by Robert Sherwood. Directed by Gregory Ratoff. Screenplay by William Hurlbutt and Michael Blankfort. From the novel Legacy *by Charles Bonner. Film editor, Francis D. Lyon. Art director, Rudolph Sternad. Director of photography, Peverell Marley. Associate producer, Gordon S. Griffith. Running time, 81 minutes.*

THE STORY

Emilie Gallatin *(Ingrid Bergman),* a French governess, comes to America and enters the employ of Adam and Molly Stoddard *(Warner Baxter* and *Fay Wray).* A quick attachment springs up between Emilie and the four Stoddard sons, Jack, David, Chris and Phillip *(Billy Ray, Steven Muller, Wallace Chadwell* and *Bobby Walberg).* Emilie also finds herself greatly admiring their father. When Adam's wife dies and financial misfortune overtakes him, he is forced to revamp his and the boys' lives in straitened circumstances, and Emilie has to return to France. But Adam and the boys never forget her, and when Adam's fortunes are finally restored, after some years of relative poverty, Emilie returns to the household. The boys are now grown, and Jack *(Richard Denning),* David *(Johnny Downs),* Chris *(Robert Shaw)* and Phillip *(Charles Lind)* are delighted, along with their father, to have her back. David brings home a pretty young wife, Hester *(Susan Hayward),* who shortly proves to be a troublemaker and a dangerous flirt.

Flighty, irresponsible and malicious, Hester

With Johnny Downs and Warner Baxter

soon wreaks havoc in the household. Emilie now fully realizes that she has always been in love with Adam, who seems to register no more than warm friendship toward her. When Emilie finds Hester in the bedroom of her brother-in-law, Jack, whom Hester has been attempting to seduce, Emilie hastily substitutes herself to save Adam the anguish of knowing that one of his sons has been cuckolding the other. Adam finds Emilie and Jack together and is upset. Hester goes scot-free briefly, but is finally exposed, and then Adam realizes that in fact he does return Emilie's long-standing love.

REVIEWS

Bosley Crowther in The New York Times:

It is blessed with the talented Ingrid Bergman in the leading and only significant role. Miss

With Warner Baxter (center) and the "sons": Billy Ray, Steven Muller, Wallace Chadwell and Bobby Walberg

With Richard Denning

Bergman, as the governess, does manage in a restrained and understanding performance to convey the devotion of a woman for the boys whom she helps to man's estate and from her alone does one catch a sincere emotional response.

Howard Barnes in the New York Herald Tribune:

Ingrid Bergman lends her great talents to an inferior film. . . . The offering finds the Swedish actress as knowing and glamorous as ever, but it never gets to first base as entertainment unless she is on screen . . . a dull adaptation of a rambling family saga . . . it never succeeds in being halfway dramatically convincing unless Miss Bergman is in there exerting her magic. . . . Miss Bergman, I am happy to report, is as undaunted as ever by a silly story. Her portrayal of the governess is completely believable and engaging . . . what she does is always filled with meaning and artistry, in spite of a bad script and indifferent direction. Surely a gift such as hers deserves a far better break than it has been given so far in Hollywood. [The film] is a torpid show, electrified at times by Miss Bergman's magnificent acting.

Cecelia Ager in PM:

It's got an old-fashioned background and an old-fashioned story, too, in which black is black and good is good and there are just two kinds of women and love is strictly spiritual, and then there's the other thing, shush. The old-fashioned background is sincere and so is Ingrid Bergman as the good kind of woman.

Walt. in Variety:

Under able guidance of Gregory Ratoff, Miss Bergman turns in a persuasive and sympathetic performance that indicates she could hit substantial boxoffice rating with more frequent assignments.

Archer Winsten in the New York Post:

Miss Bergman is such a wholesome and healthy-looking individual that it seems too much to hope that she could be an actress of taste and sensitivity also. But that is exactly what she establishes . . . beyond any question.

With Warner Baxter

Rage in Heaven

Metro-Goldwyn-Mayer, 1941

CAST

Robert Montgomery, Ingrid Bergman, George Sanders, Lucile Watson, Oscar Homolka, Philip Merivale, Matthew Boulton, Aubrey Mather, Frederic Worlock, Francis Compton, Gilbert Emery, Ludwig Hart.

CREDITS

Produced by Gottfried Reinhardt. Directed by W. S. Van Dyke II. Screenplay by Christopher Isherwood and Robert Thoeren. Based on the novel by James Hilton. Cameraman: Oliver Marsh. Musical score: Bronislau Kaper. Film editor: Harold Kress. Running time, 85 minutes.

THE STORY

Philip Monrell (Robert Montgomery), heir to an English industrial fortune, is an unstable psychotic who has escaped from a French mental hospital, where he was briefly confined without the knowledge of his mother in England, Mrs. Monrell (Lucile Watson). Philip returns to England and meets Stella Bergen (Ingrid Bergman), his mother's secretary-companion. He begins courting Stella, and she is carried away by his charm and warmth, and imagines herself in love.

After they marry, Philip's manic-depressive psychosis begins revealing itself in small ways. He is possessively jealous of his lovely wife, and when his friend Ward Andrews *(George Sanders)* comes to visit, Philip develops deep inferiority feelings in relation to Ward, whose robust mental and physical health grates on Philip's insecurities. Philip in a fit of manic bravado attempts to take over the family factory and proves so inept and paranoid that he incites a riot among the employees. Ward and the increasingly worried Stella come to his aid, and thanks to Ward's tact and cool-headedness the riot is averted. Philip is now insanely jealous of Ward and attempts to kill him by pushing him off a tower while they are inspecting the factory.

Ward by now has become suspicious of Philip and there is tension. Stella tries constantly to make Philip feel loved and secure, but he begins to torment her and accuse her of carrying on a love affair with Ward behind his back. His behavior becomes so erratic that Stella is soon afraid of him and flees the house. Philip's sick mind then collapses entirely, and he devises a scheme whereby he will kill himself and frame Ward for his "murder." Prior to his death he stages a loud quarrel with Ward which others overhear. He then commits suicide by attaching a knife to the frame of a door and leaning against it. Ward is tried for the "murder" and convicted. Frantically, Stella seeks evidence of Philip's plan and thanks to the Paris psychiatrist, Doctor Rameau *(Oscar Homolka)* who had treated Philip, she obtains it just in time to save Ward from execution.

REVIEWS

Bosley Crowther in The New York Times:

As the wife, Ingrid Bergman plays with a warm and sincere intensity which is deeply affecting.

Howard Barnes in the New York Herald Tribune:

Ingrid Bergman . . . gives a compelling impersonation of a young woman who is married to a lunatic. She has had little help from the lines or W. S. Van Dyke's direction, but she creates something of a mood of terror single-handed. If our screen keeps overlooking her great talent much longer, it will be a really black mark against it.

William R. Weaver in the Motion Picture Herald:

The film . . . combines appeal to intellect with material for devotees of the melodramatic, han-

With George Sanders

With Robert Montgomery

dling the equations in both departments with skill and effectiveness. . . . Ingrid Bergman enacts the wife whose happiness [Robert Montgomery] wrecks by his jealousy, misunderstanding and persecution.

Flin. in Variety:

[The film] is not very exciting, for all of its homicidal tension. Such realities as the film suggests come from Miss Bergman, whose portrayal of the wife is replete with well-acted and convincing scenes.

Eileen Creelman in the New York Sun:

Because of Ingrid Bergman's clear beauty, shining like a light through any picture in which she appears, the film is unusual . . . [She] some-

how holds the film together, turning a melodrama into a poignant story about a girl who finds her husband is insane. . . . *Rage in Heaven* is a heavy film, worth seeing for the glow and beauty of Ingrid Bergman.

Cecelia Ager in PM:

Psychological cases do not just grow on successful ladies' magazine writers' well-oiled typewriters. However, throbbing triangle stories do and that's what *Rage in Heaven* is. With Ingrid Bergman as the woman, it's got a far lovelier and more sensitive apex than its hackneyed story and petty philosophy deserve. George Sanders is noble as the noble other man and the script writers developed Mr. Montgomery's jealousy with nice acceleration.

With Robert Montgomery and
George Sanders

With Oscar Homolka

With Spencer Tracy

Dr. Jekyll and Mr. Hyde

Metro-Goldwyn-Mayer, 1941

CAST

Spencer Tracy, Ingrid Bergman, Lana Turner, Ian Hunter, Donald Crisp, Barton MacLane, C. Aubrey Smith, Sara Allgood, Peter Godfrey, Frederic Worlock, William Tannen, Frances Robinson, Denis Green, Billy Bevan, Forrester Harvey, Lumsden Hare, Lawrence Grant, John Barclay.

CREDITS

Produced and directed by Victor Fleming. Screenplay by John Lee Mahin, based on the story by Robert Louis Stevenson. Film editor: Harold Kress. Art director: Cedric Gibbons. Cameraman: Joseph Ruttenberg. Running time: 127 minutes.

THE STORY

Dr. Harry Jekyll (Spencer Tracy) is a London doctor of the 1880s with advanced experimental ideas. He seeks to isolate the good and evil factors in man. He is in love with, and affianced to, Beatrix Emery (Lana Turner), whose father, Sir Charles Emery (Donald Crisp), has increasing reservations about Jekyll's suitability as a son-in-law. Sir Charles indicates to Jekyll that he finds the physician's toying with matters of good and evil, however scientific his reasons, a reprehensible and mischievous avocation. Later, Sir Charles takes Beatrix abroad, hoping that she will forget Jekyll. Jekyll rescues a low-born girl, Ivy Peterson (Ingrid Bergman), from an assailant and takes her home. There Ivy tries to seduce him, and though Jekyll doesn't take advantage of his opportunity, the memory of the girl's seductive charms lingers in his mind.

With Lana Turner and Spencer Tracy

Later, with his preparations completed, Jekyll drinks a chemical that isolates the good and evil in his own nature, and he emerges as Mr. Hyde, the darker side of Harry Jekyll's dual nature. As Hyde he goes in search of Ivy, and cows her into submission. An evil relationship develops between them which undermines Ivy's nervous system, as Hyde beats and otherwise mistreats her. Ivy visits Dr. Jekyll, not realizing he is Hyde, and shows him her injuries and asks his advice. He

As the barmaid

promises her she will be free of Hyde but later, having metamorphosed again into Hyde, he seeks her out and murders her.

The doctor now finds himself shifting from Jekyll to Hyde spontaneously, without benefit of the potion, and he becomes increasingly alarmed. When Beatrix and her father return, he tries to alert her to the danger. Eventually he kills Sir Charles while under the Hyde influence, and he himself is killed battling the police. When he dies, his countenance reverts from evil Hyde features to those of Jekyll.

REVIEWS

Frank Leyendecker in Film Bulletin:

Miss Bergman's finely-shaded performance is the equal of Spencer Tracy's great tour-de-force.

Howard Barnes in the New York Herald Tribune:

Miss Bergman is so knowing and beautiful as the guttersnipe who inspires the doctor to play God that it is hard to think of any role that she could not be supreme in on the screen.

T.S. in The New York Times:

As the luckless barmaid pursued and tortured by an evil she could not understand, the young Swedish actress proves again that a shining talent can sometimes lift itself above an impossibly written role. . . . Of all the actors, only Miss Bergman has emerged with some measure of honor.

Cecelia Ager in PM:

[The film] is handsome, stuffy, pompous hoke, with nothing new to say and therefore no reason, save hunger, to say it again. Indeed, to rattle its decent Victorian bones today is most unkind. For it turns out they're not bones at all, just hollow clumps of papier-mâché . . . Mr. Hyde does go a little far; he kills a few people.

With Spencer Tracy

But at least he waits till the end of the picture to kill Ingrid Bergman, so everybody has a good chance to gaze upon her lovely face.

Norton Mockridge in the
New York World-Telegram:

There are many intriguing moments. They range from the breathtaking scene between Tracy and Miss Bergman in her bedroom (easily the most sensuous, censor-tempting of the year) to Jekyll's dramatic revelation of his dual personality to his friend Doctor Lanyon. The acting, with the exception of portions of Tracy's Mr.

Hyde, is outstanding. But Ingrid Bergman . . . is especially captivating. Whether attempting a seduction of Dr. Jekyll or shrinking in frenzied horror before the monstrous Hyde, she displays a canny combination of charm, understanding, restraint and sheer acting ability.

In Life:

Pictorially it is well worth a look at such moments when the purity of Lana Turner, who plays Jekyll's fiancée, is symbolized by white flowers and Ingrid Bergman lies in a mud puddle to indicate the baser nature of Mr. Hyde.

With Patrick J. Kelly and Rita Carlyle

Casablanca

Warner Brothers, 1942

CAST

Humphrey Bogart, Ingrid Bergman, Paul Henreid, Claude Rains, Conrad Veidt, Sydney Greenstreet, Peter Lorre, S. Z. Sakall, Madeleine Le Beau, Dooley Wilson, Joy Page, John Qualen, Leonid Kinsky, Helmut Dantine, Curt Bois, Marcel Dalio, Corinna Mura, Ludwig Gruning, Ilka Gruning, Charles La Torre, Frank Puglia, Dan Seymour.

CREDITS

Produced by Hal B. Wallis. Directed by Michael Curtiz. Screenplay by Julius J. and Philip G. Epstein and Howard Koch from the play Everybody Comes to Rick's by Murray Burnett and Joan Alison. Director of photography, Arthur Edeson. Music by Max Steiner. Film editor, Owen Marks. Songs: "As Time Goes By" by Herman Hupfeld; "Knock on Wood" by M. K. Jerome and Jack Scholl. Running time, 102 minutes.

NOTE

The picture opened originally at Thanksgiving time, 1942, and went into general release in late January, 1943. Its correct year is technically 1942.

THE STORY

In the period following the fall of France in 1940, refugees from the Nazis come from all over Europe to Casablanca, where they try to secure exit visas to Lisbon and America. One of the favorite refugee haunts in Casablanca is the Cafe Americain, owned by Rick Blaine (Humphrey Bogart). Rick has had a checkered past, having been with the Loyalists in the Spanish Civil War and having smuggled arms to Ethiopia. His reputation is enigmatic, and he tips his hand to no one.

The German authorities send Major Heinrich Strasser (Conrad Veidt) to Casablanca. He has been told to find the killers of two German

With Sydney Greenstreet

couriers who were carrying the much-sought-after letters of transit, in this case for two persons. An adventurer, Ugarte *(Peter Lorre)*, who has obtained the letters, persuades Rick to hide them for him, but Ugarte gets arrested and later killed, leaving the letters in Rick's hands. Captain Louis Renault *(Claude Rains)*, the Casablanca Prefect of Police, is cooperating with the Germans though he is not pro-German but rather a middle-of-the-roader.

To Casablanca comes Victor Laszlo *(Paul Henreid)* an anti-Nazi underground leader and his wife Ilsa *(Ingrid Bergman)*. They are seeking visas to go to America, where Victor will continue his work. They go to Rick's nightclub, and Rick and Ilsa recognize each other. In a flashback it is

With Humphrey Bogart

revealed that Ilsa and Rick once met in Paris and fell in love. They had planned to go off together just prior to the Nazi invasion, but at the last moment Ilsa had disappeared without explanation, leaving Rick disillusioned and embittered. Señor Ferrari *(Sydney Greenstreet)* a black marketeer, is approached by the Laszlos for visas, but he sends them to Rick, whom he suspects of having the missing letters of transit. Unbeknown to her husband, Ilsa later goes to Rick and begs him for the letters of transit but Rick is still embittered over the Paris interlude and refuses. Desperate, Ilsa threatens him with a gun, but, realizing she is still in love with him, cannot go through with it. She tells Rick that when she

met him in Paris she was Laszlo's wife but believed him dead in a concentration camp. Feeling she was free to give herself to Rick, she had gone ahead with the involvement, but then had learned that her husband was still alive.

Rick and Ilsa re-pledge their love for each other, though Ilsa is determined to remain loyal to Victor, whom she respects and admires. Rick decides to trick Renault into believing that he and Ilsa are leaving for Lisbon and that he will manage Laszlo's arrest if he and Ilsa are permitted to go. Renault agrees to the scheme but when they reach the airport it is Victor whom Rick sends on the plane with Ilsa. Previously Ilsa had temporarily weakened to the point where

With Paul Henreid, Claude Rains and Humphrey Bogart

she was about to desert Victor for Rick, but Rick persuades her that in view of the importance of her husband's work, her place is with him. Major Strasser, alerted by a phone call from Captain Renault, has rushed to the airport to stop the flight but is shot by Rick. Renault, touched by Rick's gallantry in sending Ilsa off with Victor, covers up for him.

REVIEWS

Frank Leyendecker in Film Bulletin:

Ingrid Bergman, with her expressive, mobile face, is reminiscent of the youthful Garbo and she here scores an acting triumph as the loyal wife.

Howard Barnes in the New York Herald Tribune:

Ingrid Bergman [plays] the heroine with all her appealing authority and beauty.... Miss Bergman illuminates every scene in which she appears.

James Agee in The Nation:

Apparently *Casablanca*, which I must say I liked, is working up a rather serious reputation as a fine melodrama. Why? It is obviously an improvement on one of the world's worst plays; but it is not such an improvement that that is not obvious. Any doubters should review the lines of Claude Rains. Rains, Bogart, Henreid, Veidt, Lorre, Sakall ... were a lot of fun, and Ingrid Bergman was more than that; but even so, Michael Curtiz still has a twenties director's correct feeling that everything, including the camera, should move; but the camera should move for purposes other than those of a nautch-dancer, and Mr. Curtiz's bit players and atmospheric scenes are not even alien corn.

Bosley Crowther in The New York Times:

The performances of the actors are all of the first order, but especially those of Mr. Bogart and Miss Bergman in the leading roles. Mr. Bogart is, as usual, the cool, cynical, efficient and super-wise guy who operates his business strictly for profit but has a core of sentiment and idealism inside. Conflict becomes his inner character and he handles it creditably. Miss Bergman is surprisingly lovely, crisp and natural as the girl and lights the romantic passages with a warm and genuine glow.

Swedes in America

Office of War Information, 1943

CAST

Ingrid Bergman, the Charles Swensons and their family of Chisago County, Minnesota, and assorted neighbors.

CREDITS

Produced by The Office of War Information's Overseas Bureau. Presented under the supervision of Robert Riskin, Chief of the Bureau. Directed by Irving Lerner. Running time, two reels.

THE THEME

In this two-reel documentary for the Office of War Information's Overseas Motion Picture Bureau, Miss Bergman lived for a week on the 320-acre farm of Charles Swenson, 73, in Chisago County, Minnesota. Mr. Swenson and his family, being typical Americans of Swedish descent, lent themselves well to the film, which was designed primarily for propaganda distribution in Sweden. It was also shown later in Great Britain and elsewhere. During the relatively short running time, Miss Bergman watched, and in some cases participated in, such farm chores as milking, handling of the stock of brown Duroc pigs, pitching hay and feeding calves. She went on a cross-country call, on skis, with the doctor son of the family. She ate her meals with the Swensons and their six sons, attended the ladies' aid meetings at the Swedish Elim Lutheran Church of Scandia, joined the family in its daily prayers, and met the women of the Swedish farming community at the church in a homey, down-to-earth reception in which everyone was cordial and at ease. She also made a speech, in Swedish, to the "folks back home."

NOTE

Among other segments of the eleven-part OWI Overseas Bureau "Projection of America" series: Edward G. Robinson of *Little Caesar* fame, telling the true story of Chicago, and *Cowboy,*

in which the men of the West were depicted realistically as hard-working and disciplined ranch hands.

REVIEWS

In Look:

In 1853, the first Swede came up the Mississippi to discover the rolling beauty of Minnesota. Ninety years later, another Nordic, Ingrid Bergman, rediscovered the lands so poetically named by the Indians—"Minne" for water, "sota" for sky-blue. When she went there to make a movie of Swedish-Americans for distribution in Sweden by our Office of War Information, a *Look* editor and cameraman joined the trek. Snow piled in seven-foot drifts; sleighs were faster than cars; the thermometer slid from zero to 30 below. But Ingrid, mittened and ski-booted, snuggled down in Minnesota. . . . It was no grand tour, but the kind of living Ingrid likes best. Because, although Sam Wood, who directed her in *For Whom the Bell Tolls,* says she will be Hollywood's top actress by next year, she is simply and completely unaffected. Her career is acting; her personal life her own.

In The New York Times:

When Ingrid Bergman, en route back to Hollywood, stops off today in Minneapolis to spend the week at a Swedish farming community, cameramen of the Office of War Information will be along. The desire of the Swedish star to go back to the land for a week with people of her own nationality fitted in perfectly with certain OWI plans. The result will be a short subject of Miss Bergman's vacation. . . .

For Whom the Bell Tolls

Paramount, 1943

CAST

Gary Cooper, Ingrid Bergman, Akim Tamiroff, Katina Paxinou, Joseph Calleia, Vladimir Sokoloff, Arturo de Cordova, Mikhail Rasumny, Eduardo Ciannelli, Fortunio Bonanova, Duncan Renaldo, Alexander Granach, Leonid Snegoff, George Coulouris, Frank Puglia, Pedro de Cordoba, Michael Visaroff, Konstantin Shayne, Martin Garralaga, Jean Del Val, Jack Mylong, Feodor Chaliapin, Mayo Newhall, Michael Delmatoff, Antonio Vidal, Robert Tafur, Armand Roland.

CREDITS

A Sam Wood Production. Produced and directed by Sam Wood. Screenplay by Dudley Nichols from the novel by Ernest Hemingway. Executive producer, B. G. DeSylva. Director of photography, Ray Rennahan. Production designed by William Cameron Menzies. Music by Victor Young. Color by Technicolor. Technicolor color director: Natalie Kalmus. Film editors: Sherman Todd and John Link. Running time, 168 minutes.

NOTE

The powers-that-be decided, after shooting had commenced, that Vera Zorina, the original choice for the role of Maria, was not right for it. She was replaced by Miss Bergman, who had been Hemingway's choice. David O. Selznick had also pressured in her behalf. The famous "sleeping bag" sequence featuring Miss Bergman and Gary Cooper was regarded as daringly erotic in 1943, though it would register as innocent enough in the 1970s. For this performance Miss

Bergman received her first nomination for an Academy Award but lost to Jennifer Jones *(Song of Bernadette)*.

THE STORY

Robert Jordan *(Gary Cooper)*, an American idealist, is fighting for the International Brigade in the camp of the Spanish loyalists in the Civil War of 1936-1939. He is a lover of freedom, an intense admirer of Spain and its people, and regards the Loyalist cause as the right one. Jordan goes to a mountainous area near Segovia; his assignment: to blow up a strategically-located bridge. The plans call for the timing of the explosion to be linked with a Loyalist offensive. The intrigues of the watchful and treacherous Communists have made the operation a delicate and top-secret one. As his allies, Jordan enlists a band of Spanish peasant guerrillas under the leadership of El Sordo *(Joseph Calleia)*. Pablo *(Akim Tamiroff)* the band's former leader, is war-weary, cynical and untrustworthy. Pablo's woman, Pilar *(Katina Paxinou)*, is a rock of strength to the others, being richly human and right-thinking. Pablo's negative attitude leads to

With Katina Paxinou (above) and Gary Cooper

With Fortunio Bonanova, Katina Paxinou and Gary Cooper

a series of conflicts within the band which Pilar's strength and positivism resolve.

Maria *(Ingrid Bergman),* a Spanish girl who has been emotionally traumatized by the loss of her parents and a vicious gang-rape, falls in love with Jordan and he with her, and her desire to live is restored by their association.

El Sordo's small but determined band use guerrilla tactics against a troop of soldiers which has come to the mountains to ferret out and destroy them. Jordan, Maria and their cohorts reach the bridge and succeed in blowing it up, though Jordan loses his life in the process. Before he completes the operation that will demand the ultimate sacrifice, he says his farewell to Maria, in words that, despite her grief, she knows will hearten and console the rest of her days.

REVIEWS

James Agee in The Nation:

Miss Bergman not only bears a startling resemblance to an imaginable human being; she really knows how to act, in a blend of poetic grace with quiet realism which almost never appears in American pictures. Hemingway's con-ception of Maria is partly adolescent, I think, and for a while her understanding of the role seems still more so. She seems never to have dreamed that a young girl who has seen death and suffered gang rape cannot in all reason bounce into her role looking like a Palmolive ad. But in many moments of the early love stuff—in flashes of shy candor and in the pleasures of playing *femme esclave*—she does very pretty things, and later on she does some very powerful ones. Her confession of the rape is an exquisitely managed tear-jerker. Her final scene of farewell is shattering to watch. Not that it's perfect. But its sources and intention are so right, and so astonishingly out of key with the rest of the production. She seems really to have studied what a young woman might feel and look like in such a situation (not a moving picture)—half-nauseated and nine-tenths insane with grief, forced haste, and utter panic. Semi-achieved though it is, it is devastating and wonderful to see.... Gary Cooper is self-effacing and generally a little faint, like the character he plays, but the faintness has its moments of paying off, and his general support of Miss Bergman is nearly as

Ingrid Bergman on the set

good as the law will allow. . . . Of all the rumbling rumors and denials of political interference on the part of the Franco government, the Catholic church and the State Department, it has been possible chiefly to find only the clogged-drain smell which the picture bears out. Franco's ambassador tried to get the State Department to suppress it and was refused. The San Francisco consul, Francisco Amat, saw the script and objected to everything you might expect him to, and was reputedly disregarded. Adolph Zukor says, "It is a great picture, without political significance. We are not for or against anybody." Other Paramount executives have delivered lines almost as distinguished. On the question

whether the opening was delayed from March to July because Robert Jordan—pardon me, Murphy—had work to do in Spain, the State Department declines comment. There are people in Washington, however, who are not eager to tie their name to it, who say that the whole affair is "too hot to talk about." Why, is any man's guess. And how this production could possibly have offended anyone politically, except a few million powerless characters who retain some vestige of moral nerve, is beyond any guessing.

Mr. Hemingway's sleeping bag, by the way, is so discreetly used that you can never at any moment be sure who is in or out nuendo.

With Katina Paxinou (center) and
Gary Cooper (right)

Howard Barnes in the New York Herald Tribune:

While Cooper and Miss Bergman dominate most of the scenes, it strikes me that Katina Paxinou, as Pilar, the wise old Loyalist guerrilla, and Akim Tamiroff, as Pablo, her vacillating husband, turn in the best performances in the picture.

George Freedley in the
New York Morning Telegraph:

[The picture] is certainly one hour too long, despite the superb photography and the decorative appearance of Ingrid Bergman in Technicolor. The cinema audiences for the first time will get the full impact of her beauty. . . . I must admit, however, that I grew intensely bored at Sam Wood's handling of the interminable love scenes between Miss Bergman and Cooper.

Eileen Creelman in the New York Sun:

Miss Bergman's glowing beauty of work, as well as appearance, gives the film its few poignant moments.

With Gary Cooper and Katina Paxinou

Gaslight

Metro-Goldwyn-Mayer, 1944

CAST

Charles Boyer, Ingrid Bergman, Joseph Cotten, Dame May Whitty, Angela Lansbury, Barbara Everest, Emil Rameau, Edmund Brean, Halliwell Hobbes, Tom Stevenson, Heather Thatcher, Lawrence Naismith, John Gimpel.

CREDITS

Produced by Arthur Hornblow, Jr. Directed by George Cukor. Screenplay by John Van Druten, Walter Reisch and John L. Balderston. Based on the play Angel Street by Patrick Hamilton. Cameraman: Joseph Ruttenberg. Music: Bronislau Kaper. Editor: Ralph E. Winters. Running time, 114 minutes.

NOTE

Under George Cukor's able directorial guidance, Miss Bergman won her first Academy Award for her performance in this film.

THE STORY

Gregory Anton (Charles Boyer), a suave and charming pianist, woos and wins Paula Alquist (Ingrid Bergman) while she is holidaying in Italy. He then suggests that they go to London and reopen a house left her by her aunt, who was mysteriously murdered there some time before.

At first they are very happy. Then a series of odd happenings ensue. Slowly, by subtle suggestion, Gregory begins to undermine Paula's self-confidence and peace of mind, and eventually she begins to doubt her own sanity. He keeps reminding her that she has become shockingly forgetful of late, and takes her to task for

With Charles Boyer

With Charles Boyer

With Joseph Cotten

minor transgressions which become ever more serious. When she registers fear and then hysteria under the growing pressure, he shows her only contempt and icy disapproval. His once-tender and affectionate manner grows ever more icy; he accuses Paula of stealing items and then forgetting where she has put them. Then he keeps her confined to the house. For some time Paula persuades herself that Gregory is merely disciplining her thoughtlessness and concerning himself with her well-being. Then doubts begin to come.

Meanwhile, Brian Cameron (Joseph Cotten), a Scotland Yard detective, has been alerted to Anton's activities, watches the house constantly, grows increasingly suspicious as to the goings-on inside, and reopens the case of Paula's aunt's unsolved murder. After he has all his facts, Cameron tells Paula that evidence points to Gregory as the murderer of her aunt. It develops that

Gregory had wished to return to the house to continue his hunt for the aunt's missing jewelry, which he had searched for unsuccessfully at the time of the murder. While Gregory is upstairs ransacking the house for the jewels (Paula now realizes that the night sounds she used to hear were *not* in her mind, as Gregory had always insisted), Cameron and his men set a trap for him. Gregory is captured and bound. Alone with Paula in the room for a brief spell, he begs her to help him get free, but she, enraged at what he has done to her for months, taunts him with his own methods and scornfully refuses to help him.

REVIEWS

Frank Leyendecker in Film Bulletin:

Miss Bergman is superb in her nerve-wracking part. Her sympathetic and emotional performance cannot fail to hold the spectator engrossed.

With Charles Boyer and
Barbara Everest

Bosley Crowther in The New York Times:

The study is wholly concerned with the obvious endeavors of a husband to drive his wife slowly mad. And with Mr. Boyer doing the driving in his best dead-pan hypnotic style, while the flames flicker strangely in the gas-jets and the mood music bongs with heavy threats, it is no wonder that Miss Bergman goes to pieces in a most distressing way. Both of these popular performers play their roles right to the hilt.

Howard Barnes in the New York Herald Tribune:

Miss Bergman contributes a lovely and pathetic portrait of the near-victim.

Kahn in Variety:

Director George Cukor has kept the film at an even pace and has been responsible for the film lacking the ten-twent-thirt element that has been a factor in the stage play. It is an apparently expensive production in the usual Metro tradition and Boyer . . . Miss Bergman . . . and Cotten have given carefully studied, restrained performances.

Jim O'Connor in the New York Journal-American:

Ingrid Bergman, one of the finest actresses in filmdom, gives the performance of her career to date . . . under the hypnotic spell of Boyer, Miss Bergman flames in passion and flickers in depression until the audience . . . becomes rigid in its seats.

Archer Winsten in the New York Post:

[Miss Bergman's] mingling of love, terror and the growing sense of her own mind's failure represents one of the better achievements of the season.

Leo Mishkin in the New York Morning Telegraph:

Monsieur Boyer and Miss Bergman, the former with his basso profundo voice and the latter with her magnificent ability, make the most out of the roles . . . riveting your attention on them all the way through.

Alton Cook in the New York World-Telegram:

Ingrid Bergman flings herself into the role with that headlong abandon that no other girl on the screen right now can manage without letting emotion slip off into hysteria.

The Bells of St. Mary's

RKO Radio, 1945

CAST

Bing Crosby, Ingrid Bergman, Henry Travers, William Gargan, Ruth Donnelly, Joan Carroll, Martha Sleeper, Rhys Williams, Dickie Tyler, Una O'Connor, Bobby Fresco, Aina Constant, Gwen Crawford, Matt McHugh, Edna Wonacott, Jimmy Crane, Minerva Urecal, Pietro Sosso, Cora Shannon, Joseph Palma, Jimmy Dundee, Dewey Robinson.

With Bing Crosby

CREDITS

Produced and directed by Leo McCarey for Rainbow Productions. Screenplay by Dudley Nichols from a story by Leo McCarey. Cameraman: George Barnes. Musical score by Robert Emmett Dolan. Songs by Douglas Farber-A. Emmett Adams; John Burke-James Van Heusen; Grant Clarke-George W. Meyer. Film editor: Harry Marker. Running time, 126 minutes.

THE STORY

Father O'Malley *(Bing Crosby)* is assigned to a new parish with a parochial school that is run-down and needs rehabilitation. Presiding over the students is Sister Benedict *(Ingrid Bergman),* an individualist who believes that prayer solves all problems and that rote gets things done. The priest and the nun find themselves arguing over ways and means at first—Father O'Malley thinks Sister Benedict rigid and old-fashioned and she thinks him too loose and permissive—but gradually, in the face of the common problems, they become allies. Sister Benedict coaches a frail, put-upon boy, Eddie *(Dickie Tyler),* in the manly art of self-defense, complete with boxing gloves and gym session.

Father O'Malley tries to bring a happier ad-justment to a lonely little girl, Patsy *(Joan Carroll),* whom he tutors. Patsy's flighty, estranged parents *(Martha Sleeper* and *William Gargan)* have left her to her own devices at the school, but are gradually made to realize their responsibilities by the priest and the nun. The small fry put on a nativity play as part of the Christmas pageant. Mr. Bogardus *(Henry Travers),* a wealthy industrialist but a mean old curmudgeon, is inveigled into giving up the building he owns for a new school.

Sister Benedict's health fails, and it is found necessary to remove her from her post for a less demanding assignment. She does not realize the extent to which her health has deteriorated and it is concealed from her by Father O'Malley and the nuns. She is deeply hurt, thinking that her work has gone unappreciated, but at the fadeout she is made to feel the admiration of Father O'Malley and her co-workers in terms that will cheer her always.

REVIEWS

Bosley Crowther in The New York Times:

In planning this project. . . . Leo McCarey, who also planned *Going My Way,* yielded too

102

much to the temptation of trying to copy a success. He followed too closely the pattern of his previous delightful film [*Going My Way*], with the lone exception of including a character of genuine scope. Father O'Malley is generally consistent (and played by Bing Crosby, what else could he be?), but Sister Benedict has not the veracity of her counterpart character, which was played by Barry Fitzgerald. She is much too precisely sugar-coated, too eagerly contrived, and she goes in for certain gymnastics which are just on the edge of being cheap. As a consequence, *The Bells of St. Mary's,* although a plenteous and sometimes winning show, lacks the charm of its predecessor—and that comparison cannot be escaped. . . . In the role of Sister Benedict, Ingrid Bergman is exquisitely serene, radiantly beautiful and soft-spoken—the perfect picture of an idealized nun. And there are moments (*not* the close-up shot of her praying) in which she glows with tenderness and warmth. But—more the script's fault than Miss Bergman's—her holiness smacks of Hollywood, and certainly she seems much too youthful to be the head of a parochial school.

Howard Barnes in the New York Herald Tribune:

Leo McCarey has pursued a hazardous path with surefooted . . . serenity. [The film] challenges comparison with the director's brilliant *Going My Way* but it does not beg it. Bing Crosby reappears as the wise Father O'Malley and is confronted with somewhat similar situations, [but] the chief kinship of two fine pictures is one of sincerity, feeling and artistry. Once again a theme of spirited depth and delicate human equations has been wrought into a taut and revealing screen entertainment. Rarely has so beautiful an equilibrium been established between treatment and performance. McCarey and Dudley Nichols have fashioned a consummate continuity, making a rich tapestry of small, significant dramatic incidents and illuminating it with eloquent speech. The former has staged the work with heart as well as imagination. Meanwhile, Crosby and Miss Bergman, with whom he is felicitously paired in this instance, play the leading roles with supreme assurance and persuasion. . . . Miss Bergman brings warmth and extraordinary versatility to the part of the nun. Her stubborn insistence on marks rather than intellectual ability makes her the sternest of school mistresses, her boxing lessons reveal the nun as intensely human, and the fortitude with which she takes dismissal, not knowing that it is

With Bing Crosby and nuns

With Martha Sleeper and Joan Carroll

a matter of her health, springs a series of poignant coincidences.... Together (Crosby and Miss Bergman) avoid any touch of saccharine sanctimony and give their somewhat drab garb a luminous quality.... *The Bells of St. Mary's* is inspiring, in the correct sense of that word. It is a picture to be welcomed in this yuletide or any other season.

In Cue:

The general result is an uneven picture—beginning with sparkle and bounce but devolving later into entertainment fits and starts as the plot tries to make up its mind in which direction to go. Bing Crosby as Father O'Malley does an excellent job as the helpful priest and sings three songs, while Ingrid Bergman as the unbelievably young Mother Superior struggles with a difficult role and sings one song.

With director Leo McCarey and
Bing Crosby

104

With Gregory Peck

Spellbound

Selznick-United Artists, 1945

CAST

Ingrid Bergman, Gregory Peck, Michael Chekhov, Jean Acker, Donald Curtis, Rhonda Fleming, Leo G. Carroll, Norman Lloyd, John Emery, Paul Harvey, Steven Geray, Erskine Sanford, Janet Scott, Victor Kilian, Wallace Ford, Dave Willock, Bill Goodwin, George Meader, Matt Moore, Harry Brown, Art Baker, Regis Toomey, Joel Davis, Clarence Straight, Teddy Infuht, Richard Bartell, Addison Richards, Ed Fielding.

CREDITS

Produced by David O. Selznick. Directed by Alfred Hitchcock. Screenplay by Ben Hecht. Adaptation by Angus MacPhail from the novel The House of Doctor Edwards, *by Francis Beeding. Music by Miklos Rozsa. Surrealistic dream sequence by Salvador Dali. Running time, 111 minutes.*

THE STORY

Doctor Constance Peterson *(Ingrid Bergman),* a young psychiatrist in a fashionable sanitarium, becomes suspicious when the newly-arrived head of the mental hospital turns out to be "J.B." *(Gregory Peck)* a very young man who seems strange in his behavior and reveals himself gradually to be an amnesiac. It becomes increasingly apparent that "J.B." at some earlier point had assumed the identity of the incoming sanitarium head and possibly murdered him. When "J.B." begins twitching and grimacing and waxes pale at the sight of fork marks on a tablecloth, Constance realizes that he may be not only homicidal and amnesiacal but also mentally ill.

Aware that his imposture is being uncovered, "J.B." flees, and Constance, who is gradually falling in love with him, follows, and persuades him to accompany her upstate to the home of

With Gregory Peck

With Michael Chekhov, Regis Toomey and Erskine Sanford

With Gregory Peck

her friend and teacher *(Michael Chekhov)* whose aid she seeks in diagnosing "J.B.'s" case. The kindly doctor tries to persuade her that she may well be involved with a dangerous maniac, but she persists in her theory that the young man is the victim of a guilt complex built upon some long-gone childhood incident.

"J.B." now tells her that he has fallen in love with her, as she has with him, and they set out together to find the secret of his past. Confused, his memory gone, "J.B." does frightening things, standing by her bed with a knife in his hands while she lies sleeping, and they travel, always one jump ahead of the police, seeking his past in locations that may jog his memory. In a climactic ski ride down a slope where he had been seen with the doctor he had replaced, "J.B." recaptures the memory that sets him free: he had inadvertently killed his brother in childhood by sliding down an incline and pushing the other boy onto some protruding spikes that impaled him.

With her lover now liberated and his mind and memory restored, Constance, guided by clues given her by "J.B." while under analysis,

sets out to find the real murderer. The search leads her eventually back to the sanitarium, where she tricks Doctor Murchison *(Leo G. Carroll)* into an admission that he had followed the murdered man and "J.B." to the ski slope and had shot the doctor from behind. Shocked by the sudden death, "J.B." who had been subconsciously laboring for years under the emotional strain of the childhood incident, had gone into a mental trauma in which he subconsciously assumed the guilt of the murder and substituted himself for the other doctor at the sanitarium. Doctor Murchison threatens Constance with a gun, but she coolly backs out of his office, and he then turns the gun on himself. Constance and "J.B.," the unhappy past behind them, plan a life together.

REVIEWS

In Time:

The script allows Miss Bergman to do very little except tensely beg her lover to remember his boyhood. By flexing his jaw muscles and narrowing his eyes, Peck does his best to register the fact that all is not well with him. But despite

With Gregory Peck

the drag of the psychoanalytical theme, director Hitchcock's deft timing and sharp, imaginative camera work raise *Spellbound* well above the routine of Hollywood thrillers. Again and again he injects excitement into an individual scene with his manipulation of such trivia as a crack of light under a door, a glass of milk, or the sudden wailing of a locomotive whistle.

Frank Leyendecker in Film Bulletin:

Miss Bergman, who is serene and completely convincing as the psychoanalyst who falls in love with her patient, again proves herself one of the screen's finest actresses.

Howard Barnes in the New York Herald Tribune:

The secret recesses of the mind are explored with brilliant and terrifying effect. . . . That master of overt melodrama, Alfred Hitchcock, has

turned to the subtleties of the subconscious . . . with Ben Hecht's crafty scenario and compelling performances by Ingrid Bergman and Gregory Peck, the work is a masterful psychiatric thriller. . . . Hecht has filled his script with eloquence as well as excitement. [Miss Bergman] gives one of her most serene and artful portrayals.

Bosley Crowther in The New York Times:

This writer has had little traffic with practitioners of psychiatry or with the twilight abstractions of their science, so we are not in a position to say whether Ingrid Bergman, who plays one in her latest film, *Spellbound*, is typical of such professionals or whether the methods she employs would yield results. But this we can say with due authority: if all psychiatrists are as charming as she—and if their attentions to all their patients are as fruitful as hers are to Gregory

108

With Gregory Peck

Peck, who plays a victim of amnesia in this fine film—then psychiatry deserves such popularity as this picture most certainly will enjoy. For Miss Bergman and her brand of treatment, so beautifully demonstrated here, is a guaranteed cure for what ails you, just as much as it is for Mr. Peck. It consists of her winning personality, softly but insistently suffused through a story of deep emotional content; of her ardent sincerity, her lustrous looks and her easy ability to toss off glibly a line of talk on which most girls would choke. In other words, lovely Miss Bergman is both the doctor and the prescription in this film. She is the single stimulation of dramatic logic and audience belief . . . the firm texture of the narrative, the flow of continuity and dialogue, the shock of the unexpected, the scale of image—all are happily here.

Saratoga Trunk

Warner Brothers, 1945

CAST

Gary Cooper, Ingrid Bergman, Flora Robson, Jerry Austin, Florence Bates, John Warburton, John Abbott, Curt Bois, Ethel Griffies, Minor Watson, Louis Payne, Fred Essler, Adrienne D'Ambricourt, Helen Freeman, Sophie Huxley, Marla Shelton, Sarah Edwards, Jacqueline DeWit, Thurston Hall, William B. Davidson, Theodore Von Eltz, Glenn Strange, Monte Blue, Georges Renavent, Alice Fleming, Alan Bridge, Ruby Dandridge, Ralph Dunn.

CREDITS

Produced by Hal B. Wallis. Directed by Sam Wood. Screenplay by Casey Robinson. Based on the novel by Edna Ferber. Cameraman: Ernest Haller. Music by Max Steiner. Film editor: Lawrence Butler. Running time, 135 minutes.

THE STORY

Clio Dulaine (Ingrid Bergman), the half-creole illegitimate daughter of a New Orleans aristocrat, returns to New Orleans from Paris after her mother's death to revenge herself on her father's snobbish family. She is accompanied on her flamboyant hegira by her attendants, Angelique (Flora Robson) and Cupidon (Jerry Austin), a dwarf. Once in New Orleans, Clio encounters a Texas gambler, Clint Maroon (Gary Cooper) and flirts with him off and on, while pursuing her principal aim: the humiliation of the Dulaines. Eventually she prevails on the family to pay her $10,000 to get out of town, but she leaves a humiliating set of conditions behind her, among them that her mother shall be buried in the Dulaine family plot.

Maroon, who despite himself has become emotionally involved with Clio, is disenchanted with her self-centered opportunism and takes off for Saratoga Springs, stamping ground for millionaires and adventurers of all persuasions. The

With Gary Cooper

money-mad Clio eventually follows him there, posing as a French noblewoman, and determines to snag a rich husband. Mrs. Coventry Bellop *(Florence Bates)*, a *haute monde* contact, sees through Clio's imposture, investigates her in New Orleans and Paris, and offers to help her land wealthy railroad tycoon Bart Van Steed *(John Warburton)*, but Clio scorns her help. As she admires Clio's spirit, Mrs. Bellop offers to help her without the post-marriage cut she originally asked. Clint is half-amused, half-annoyed at Clio's machinations among the society toffs.

When Van Steed's mother, Clarissa *(Ethel Griffies)*, appears at Saratoga and challenges Clio's background, Mrs. Bellop sticks up for her. Meanwhile Clio is making progress with Van Steed, who asks her hand in marriage, despite the fact he knows her background. Clint gets involved with Van Steed's railroad war with other tycoons over a branch line called The Saratoga Trunk, and goes out to fight railroad sharks, getting wounded in a fierce battle in which two

With Jerry Austin and Flora Robson

With Gary Cooper

trains collide at top speed. When he returns to the hotel in bad shape, Clio realizes she loves him and gives up the millionaire.

NOTE

Saratoga Trunk was made between February and May 1943 but withheld from general release. It was shown for the next two years in Army camps overseas. First shown to theatre audiences in November 1945, it went into general release in March 1946. This was one of several Warner pictures made in 1943-44 and not released until 1946-47, among them *Devotion* with Olivia De Havilland, *My Reputation* with Barbara Stanwyck, and *The Two Mrs. Carrolls* with Miss Stanwyck and Humphrey Bogart, the last being a 1947 release.

REVIEWS

Bosley Crowther in The New York Times:

The Warners' bedizened and bulging *Saratoga Trunk* was delivered yesterday to the Hollywood [Theatre, New York] with the usual clatter and bang. And out of it spilled such a rummage of cinematic gew-gaws and antiques that it is certain to fascinate those persons who delight in poring over gaudy junk. For the Warners have taken the novel which Edna Ferber wrote, a novel of high romantic polish and maddening emptiness underneath, and have given it visualization in the grand, flashy, empty Hollywood style. They have taken Miss Ferber's period story of a beautiful creole girl, of a long, lanky conman from Texas, and their traffic with high society swells and have made it appear just precisely the fictitious romance that it is. Indeed, they have decked out their fable with so many familiar film festoons that one cannot seriously regard it as anything but a manufactured show. . . . It has plenty of plushness in the splendor of its decor and a studiedly ostentatious and insistent musical score. But it lacks a logical pattern of drama and character—and that the competent playing of Gary Cooper and Ingrid Bergman cannot supply. The money-mad creole lady whom Miss Bergman elegantly plays is a stereotyped screen adventuress with a dozen antecedents

With Gary Cooper

one could name, and Mr. Cooper's Texas gambler is a familiarly mechanical picaroon.

Unfortunately most of the action takes place between these two, and is played to such tedious extremities that the interest there is in it is dulled. Miss Bergman gives ample surface evidence of a coquettish, impulsive miss and looks quite fetching with dark hair and eyebrows, but there is no genuine spirit in her act. It is hard to accept this proper lady as the willful courtesan she is supposed to be, and Mr. Cooper, while pleasantly roguish, has an air of substantial piety.

Howard Barnes in the New York Herald Tribune:

The stars will make the work a resounding smash and they well deserve to do so. Even when they are involved with a clutter of staccato melodrama, or in interludes of burlesque social satire, they move serenely and assuredly through the sequences. Miss Bergman, become brunette and willful for this occasion, is magnificent, playing with a verve and versatility that would make

one think that she actually was part-creole.

In Time:

[The picture] has been packed by expert hands with practically everything a film needs for a triumphant boxoffice tour. In the top-drawer of this expensive portmanteau, Ingrid Bergman is wonderfully bewitching in a black wig and bustle and Gary Cooper drawls and sprawls in his best skin-tight cow pants. Edna Ferber's plot slides them expertly through a period-piece romance without missing one of the primary Hollywood emotions ... despite its tried-and-true formula and two-hours-plus running time, [the picture] is a glamorous double portion of consistently entertaining entertainment. . . . Ingrid Bergman is that rarity in Hollywood—a good-looking woman who can change her personality to suit her part. As Clio, freed from the virtuous nobility of her usual roles, her brilliant act of sexy razzle-dazzle makes most of Hollywood's glamor girls look like bobby-soxers.

With Cary Grant

Notorious

RKO Radio, 1946

CAST

Cary Grant, Ingrid Bergman, Claude Rains, Louis Calhern, Madame Konstantin, Ivan Triesault, Reinhold Schunzel, Moroni Olsen, Alex Minotis, Wally Brown, Ricardo Costa, Lenore Ulric, Sir Charles Mendl, Eberhard Krumschmidt, Fay Baker.

CREDITS

An Alfred Hitchcock Production for RKO release. Produced and directed by Alfred Hitchcock. Written by Ben Hecht. Director of Photography: Ted Tetzlaff. Art directors: Albert S. D'Agnostino and Carroll Clark. Music by Roy Webb. Musical director: C. Bakaleinikoff. Orchestral arrangements by Gil Grau. Miss Bergman's gowns by Edith Head. Special effects: Vernon L. Walker. Production assistant: Barbara Keon. Set decorations: Darrell Silvera, Claude Carpenter. Special effects: Vernon L. Walker. Film editor: Theron Warth. Running time, 103 minutes.

THE STORY

Alicia Huberman (Ingrid Bergman) finds herself notorious when her father is convicted as a German spy. She encounters Devlin (Cary Grant), an agent for the U.S. Government, and they fall in love. Devlin enlists her services on a dangerous mission he is about to undertake in Rio de Janeiro. He asks Alicia to contact Alexander Sebastian (Claude Rains), who had been a good friend of her father, the object being to get facts about a reportedly sinister project that Sebastian and his Nazi colleagues have in the works. As she wishes to prove herself a good American, Alicia ingratiates herself with Sebastian, who becomes enamored of her and asks her to marry him, though Sebastian's autocratic mother, Mme. Sebastian (Madame Konstantin), advises him against it. Despite her love for Devlin, Alicia agrees to contract the marriage while continuing to unearth the truth about Sebastian's secret operation. She becomes Mrs. Sebastian and at a party the newlyweds give, Alicia, acting on information she has gradually pieced together, gives Devlin the key to the wine cellar, where he discovers uranium ore samples in the bottles.

Sebastian finds Alicia and Devlin together, and

realizes that Alicia is an American spy and that it is possible Devlin may learn the whole truth: that Sebastian and his cohorts plan to manufacture atomic weapons for the next great war. Sebastian and his mother slowly poison Alicia, who finds it impossible to communicate with Devlin. Becoming suspicious, Devlin gets into the house and promises Sebastian that if he is allowed to get Alicia to a hospital he will not disclose her husband's mistake to his colleagues.

But Sebastian is found out and liquidated by his fellow-conspirators. Alicia and Devlin, their mission accomplished, plan a future together.

REVIEWS

James Agee in The Nation:

Notorious lacks many of the qualities which made the best of Alfred Hitchcock's movies so good, but it has more than enough good qualities of its own. Hitchcock has always been as

With Cary Grant and Lenore Ulric

With Claude Rains

good at domestic psychology as at thrillers, and many times here he makes a moment in a party, or a lovers' quarrel, or a mere interior shrewdly exciting in ways that few people in films seem to know. His great skill in directing women is functioning beautifully again: I think that Ingrid Bergman's performance here is the best of hers that I have seen.

Joe Pihodna in the New York Herald Tribune:

Whether the mixture of romance and suspense in *Notorious* is as explosive as it was intended to be, there is no denying the pull and ingratiating charm of the principals, Ingrid Bergman and Cary Grant. For once, Alfred Hitchcock, master of the screen thriller, has to take a back seat to the star system. More footage is given over to romance than to evil doings, an unusual turn of events in a Hitchcock film. It is better than an even money bet that the movie fans will be wanting to see more of Bergman and Grant as a team of romancers. How some of the film at the Music Hall got past the censors, especially where the pair engage in a protracted kissing scene, is hard to say. There is no gainsaying the fact that they are a very warm team indeed. They play their roles straightaway, which means everything they do is in dead earnest despite the high-flown melodramatics concocted by Ben Hecht. From now on RKO Radio Pictures will have a hard time keeping them apart. The movie-goers will be shouting for more.

Bosley Crowther in The New York Times:

Mr. Hecht and Mr. Hitchcock have treated [the romantic situation] with sophistication and irony. There is nothing unreal or puritanical in their exposure of a frank, grown-up *amour*. And Miss Bergman and Mr. Grant have played it with surprising and disturbing clarity. We do not recall a more conspicuous—yet emotionally delicate—love scene on the screen than one stretch of billing and cooing that the principals play in this film—yet, withal, there is rich and real emotion expressed by Miss Bergman in her role, and the integrity of her nature as she portrays it is the prop that holds the show.

Frank Leyendecker in Film Bulletin:

Alfred Hitchcock's superb directorial skill, combined with luminous acting by Ingrid Bergman and Cary Grant, make *Notorious* a topnotch thriller. The marquee magic of these three names, plus an intriguing title, will make this one of the foremost money attractions of the season. Ben Hecht's skillful reworking of an ordinary spy tale results in a film that holds audiences spellbound and the several romantic sequences have rarely been surpassed on the screen for passionate intensity. Hitchcock, as is his wont, builds suspense slowly and steadily until he approaches a climax which will have patrons gripping the arms of their seats in excitement. . . . Ingrid Bergman's brilliant portrayal again makes her a candidate for an Academy Award and Cary Grant gives his finest screen performance to date as the Government agent torn between love and duty.

Arch of Triumph

Enterprise-United Artists, 1948

CAST

Ingrid Bergman, Charles Boyer, Charles Laughton, Louis Calhern, Roman Bohner, Stephen Bekassy, Ruth Nelson, Curt Bois, J. Edward Bromberg, Michael Romanoff, Art Smith, John Laurenz, Leon Lenoir, Franco Corsaro, Nino Pepitoni, Vladimar Rashevsky, Alvin Hammer, Jay Gilpin, Ilia Khmara, Andre Marsauden, Hazel Brooks, Byron Foulger, William Conrad, Peter Virgo, Feodor Chaliapin.

CREDITS

A David Lewis Production for the Enterprise Studios. Directed by Lewis Milestone. Screenplay by Lewis Milestone and Harry Brown, based on the novel by Erich Maria Remarque. Cameraman: Russell Metty. Musical score: Louis Gruenberg, conducted by Morris Stoloff. Musical director: Rudolph Polk. Film editor: Mario Castegnaro. Running time, 120 minutes.

THE STORY

To the Paris of 1938 come many refugees from Nazi persecution in middle Europe, among them Dr. Ravic (Charles Boyer), a former member of the Austrian underground and a surgeon. While walking on a bridge over the Seine, Ravic saves from suicide a Parisian drifter, Joan Madou (Ingrid Bergman). He goes with her to her apartment, where her lover lies dead in bed. Ravic arranges matters to disinvolve Joan from the coroner's inquest. Then he sets her up in a room and finds her a job singing at the Scheherazade,

With Charles Boyer

With Charles Boyer

where the doorman is his ex-Czarist-officer friend, Morosow (*Louis Calhern*), a wry, philosophic type. Ravic is deported, and while he is away, Joan drifts back into her former way of life. When he manages to get back to Paris, they renew their love affair and go to the Riviera, where Joan, in some ways the prisoner of her past and the tool of her emotional conditioning, flirts with a rich playboy, Alex (*Stephen Bekassy*).

Meanwhile, Ravic has sworn revenge on his enemy Haake (*Charles Laughton*), a Nazi bigwig sojourning in Paris. Haake had tortured Ravic back in Austria and killed his fiancée (*Hazel Brooks*), also a member of the Austrian underground. One night Ravic approaches Haake, who does not remember his face, and kills him. Ravic demands that Joan abandon Alex, with whom she has begun an affair, but she declares that though she loves Ravic, she doesn't want to give up Alex just yet. Later, in a fit of jealousy, Alex shoots Joan, who dies just as World War II breaks out. So much for the displaced persons and odd-men-out who live in the shadow of Paris' ironically-named Arc de Triomphe.

REVIEWS

James Agee in The Nation:

Some real talent, and a lot of desperate effort, lost in a picture God wisely forsook. If you

With Louis Calhern and Charles Boyer

With Charles Boyer

haven't lived until you've seen Bergman love Boyer, you should have stood in bed.

Lawrence J. Quirk in Movies in Boston:

Miss Bergman and Mr. Boyer rise consistently above their material, which is verbally leaden and dramatically static. Even the protean efforts of these superstars, however, cannot rescue or redeem the dismal totality. But we defy you to take your eyes off Miss Bergman or Boyer when they are on screen.

Bosley Crowther in The New York Times:

This overdrawn picture, upon which much time and coin were spent, is just a hermetically sealed love story played by beauteous Ingrid Bergman and Charles Boyer. . . . From within Lewis Milestone's roving camera, we watch love as it is made by two of the movies' most able craftsmen, repetitiously and at exceeding length. And to the inevitable question, "Is that bad?" we can only say that too much of a good thing—even of Bergman and Boyer—is too much. Even of Bergman and Boyer quarreling . . . even of Bergman and Boyer yearning towards one another in that final deathbed scene, it is all just a little too tedious when exclusively pursued at two-hours' length. That, in the end, is the trouble with *Arch of Triumph* on the screen: an over-

Ingrid Bergman singing, right

indulgence of personalized romance to the disadvantage of the broader theme. Miss Bergman and Mr. Boyer look lovely, she with her cleancut, graceful style (quite hard to reconcile with her characterization) and he with his tragic eyes and brow. Louis Calhern is amusing as the Russian and Charles Laughton is absurd as the Nazi brute. But they're none of them people in prewar Paris. They're just actors in a slow, expensive film—a film, we might add, in which a blighted romance is all that stands as the tragic symbol of a tottering world.

Otis L. Guernsey Jr. in the
New York Herald Tribune:

Bergman and Boyer are not well cast together—between them there is no unseen catalyst of personality to set off a reaction in the two-shots. Boyer overdoes the taciturn, eyebrow-raising, secretive refugee, making Bergman's

mobile features seem grotesque; and her lithe performance, always a notch or two above realism, makes him appear bored. Milestone attempts to stimulate movement with constant cutting, but in neither case is he successful. Neither he nor the stars are able to make an emotion out of a bunch of flowers, a statuette or even a deep sigh, and the abrupt excursions into melodrama are made no more believable by the occasional closeup of a gun.

In Life:

Remarque's novel deserved attention because it documented the life of a political refugee, but that is barely suggested in the movie, which contains little authentic flavor of appeasement-era Europe. Considered solely as a love story, however, [the film] is a tasteful, adult motion picture. Ingrid Bergman and . . . Charles Boyer are highly romantic as the two doomed soulmates.

Joan of Arc

Sierra Pictures-RKO Radio, 1948

CAST

Ingrid Bergman, José Ferrer, George Coulouris, Richard Derr, Ray Teal, Roman Bohnen, Selena Royle, Jimmy Lydon, Robert Barrat, Francis L. Sullivan, Rand Brooks, Nestor Paiva, Irene Rich, Gene Lockhart, Nicholas Joy, Frederic Worlock, Tom Browne Henry, Vincent Donahue, Richard Ney, Colin Keith-Johnston, Leif Erickson, John Emery, John Ireland, Ward Bond, Gregg Barton, Henry Brandon, Dennis Hoey, J. Carrol Naish, Hurd Hatfield, Cecil Kellaway, Ethan Laidlaw, Morris Ankrum, Philip Bourneuf, Sheppard Strudwick, Taylor Holmes, Stephen Roberts, Frank Puglia, Houseley Stevenson, Alan Napier, David Bond, Bill Kennedy, Victor Wood, George Zucco, Jeff Corey, John Parrish, Mary Currier, Aubrey Mather, Herbert Rudley, William Conrad, Frank Elliott, Roy Roberts, Barbara Wooddell, Greta Granstedt, Julie Faye, Marjorie Wood, Arthur Space, Eve March.

CREDITS

A Sierra Pictures presentation. Produced by Walter Wanger. Directed by Victor Fleming. Adapted from the play Joan of Lorraine by Max-

With John Ireland, John Emery,
and Ward Bond

well Anderson. *Screenplay by Maxwell Anderson
and Andrew Solt. Photographed by Joseph Val-
entine. Music by Hugo Friedhofer. Music di-
rection: Emil Newman. Arrangements: Jerome
Moross. Vocals: Charles Henderson with Roger
Wagner Choir. Art direction: Richard Day. As-
sistant director: Slavko Vorkapich. Editor: Frank
Sullivan. Special effects: Jack Cosgrove, John
Fulton. Second unit director: Horace Hough.
Color by Technicolor. Running time, 150 minutes.*

THE STORY

The plot follows the well-known outlines of
the career of the fifteenth century French saint,
Joan of Arc. It begins with the peasant girl, Joan,
in the remote village of Domremy in Lorraine.
She hears voices that tell her to go forth and
save France from the depredations of the invad-
ing English, who have taken over most of its
territory and prevented its rightful king, the Dauphin Charles VII *(José Ferrer)* from achieving his
coronation.

Joan is sent by Robert de Baudricourt *(George
Coulouris)* to the court of Charles VII at Chinon.
Charles, an ironist and a worldling, tries to trick
the maid by hiding among his courtiers while a

noble *(Richard Ney)* pretends to be the king. But
Joan makes her way with certainty to the real
king, and he is moved by her eloquence and
positivism to recruit an army to fight the English.
Joan is placed at its head and, assisted by able
French generals, she lifts the siege of Orleans
and goes on to other victories.

The people idolize her, and the army, trusting
confidently in her spiritual leadership, wins one
battle after another. The high point of her career
comes when she stands beside Charles VII at his
coronation at Rheims. But Charles is crafty, tricky
and worldly in his goals, and shortly he is capi-
talizing on the gains won for him by the Maid
to carry out his meaner schemes for acquiring
money and land. Joan, weary and disillusioned,
is captured by the English and subjected to a
series of trials, first in an ecclesiastical and then
in a civil court. Due to the machinations of cor-
rupt clergy and English political figures, she is
condemned to death at the stake.

REVIEWS

In The Times (London):

[Miss Bergman] has dignity, and in the moments when her voices speak to her and she

123

With Richard Derr and Ray Teal

finds herself caught up in a mesh of forces and motives she cannot understand, she dissolves into a radiant tenderness which breaks the arbitrary patterns of the screen down to a simpler and more effective design. . . . Mr. José Ferrer makes the Dauphin a man properly perplexed within himself.

Lawrence J. Quirk in Movies in Boston:

Miss Bergman is a radiant and sensitive Joan, replete with buoyant spiritual zeal and a healthy affirmation that sweeps king and warriors into following her lead in the liberation of their homeland. And when evil days come upon her, she is mutely eloquent in some scenes, tragically impassioned in others, and always charismatically mesmeric. Being a true star, she keeps the attention riveted on her person, not only because the story is built around her, but because she commands attention in her own right. Miss Bergman is unquestionably one of the finest actresses who have ever graced the screen. Hers is a quality so unique, so individual and so distinctive that it will never be duplicated. Nature—and Art—broke the mold after fusing and fashioning the uniquenesses of Ingrid Bergman. Delicate

poetess and sturdy peasant meet in her and blend their strengths.

Howard Barnes in the New York Herald Tribune:

Ingrid Bergman gives a rapt portrayal of the title role. Scores of principals and hundreds of extras fill in the tinted backgrounds of some two-and-a-half hours of panoply, martial alarums, betrayal and persecution. Indisputably *Joan of Arc* has size. . . . The star is at her happiest in the early stanzas. Her inspired mission to head the army of France and give the Dauphin his royal prerogatives has heart and meaning.

Bosley Crowther in The New York Times:

Out of the history and the legends of France's great national saint and out of the brilliant stuff of pageants which the bold cinematist commands, Sierra Pictures has fashioned a stupendous film . . . which moved with the pomp of a procession onto the screen. Pictorially it is one of the most magnificent films ever made, bespeaking the vast sum of money and the effort expended on it. Dramatically, it has moments of tremendous excitement and shock. And emo-

With Jose Ferrer, Gene Lockhart, and John Emery

tionally it has glimmers of the deep poignancy of the Maid.

John Mason Brown in Saturday Review:

The assets Miss Bergman brings to The Maid are many. Her body is boyish and tall; her legs slim and long. She wears armor well. The peasant's simplicity is hers. There is no resisting her goodness. Hers is an uncommon gift for making virtue interesting . . . there is a genuine effulgence about her.

In Time:

Ingrid Bergman gives Joan the unlipsticked dignity and the spiritual conviction that the story demands. Wherever Hollywood puts a stagey gloss on the scene, reminding the audience that what they are looking at is a very expensive movie set, Bergman's passionate fidelity to her part saves the day.

At the stake

Under Capricorn

Warner Brothers, 1949

CAST

Ingrid Bergman, Joseph Cotten, Michael Wilding, Margaret Leighton, Cecil Parker, Denis O'Dea, Jack Watling, Harcourt Williams, John Ruddock, Bill Shine, Victor Lucas, Ronald Adam, Francis de Wolff, G. H. Mulcaster, Olive Sloan, Maureen Delaney, Julia Lang, Betty McDermott, Roderick Lovell.

CREDITS

A Transatlantic pictures production for Warner Brothers release. Directed by Alfred Hitchcock. Screenplay by James Bridie from Hume Cronyn's adaptation of the play by John Colton and Margaret Linden and the novel by Helen Simpson. Color by Technicolor. Technicolor color director: Natalie Kalmus. Musical score by Richard Addinsell. Musical director: Louis Levy. Director of photography: Jack Cardiff. Film editor: A. S. Bates. Running time, 117 minutes.

THE STORY

The setting is Australia in 1831. Prior to the action of the story, Sam Flusky (Joseph Cotten), a groom in Ireland, had eloped with Lady Henrietta Considine (Ingrid Bergman), the daughter of his titled employer. Her brother had tried to intercept the elopement, and Sam was tried and convicted for his murder and deported to Australia. Henrietta, reduced to poverty, followed along. After his release, under a rule that allows

With Margaret Leighton and
Michael Wilding

ex-convicts a "clean slate" to begin all over again, Sam had prospered in Sydney and had become a rich landowner.

The marriage of Sam and Henrietta is not happy, and their aura is so negative that they are shunned by polite society. Henrietta has become an alcoholic and has withdrawn into herself. Milly *(Margaret Leighton),* the housekeeper at the Flusky mansion, has designs on Sam and rules the house with an iron hand, humiliating the weakened and confused Henrietta whenever she can.

Henrietta's cousin, the Honorable Charles Adare *(Michael Wilding),* comes to Australia seeking his fortune and looks up the Fluskys. Dapper and charming, he is appalled at the unhappiness and deplorable conditions in which he finds Henrietta and tries to help her. Flusky agrees, feeling that talk of old times and moving with people of her own class may bring her out of her depression. Milly insinuates to Flusky that a romance is growing between Henrietta and Charles. In fact, Charles' feelings have evolved from sympathy to love.

Milly tries to poison Henrietta and is caught in the act by Sam. She leaves the house, but comes back later to torment Sam with added insinuations about his wife and Adare. Sam is abusive to Henrietta at a society function where his humble birth makes him ill at ease, and Charles quarrels with him and is wounded. To save her husband from criminal action, Henri-

etta decides to confess a long-concealed truth: that it was she, not Sam, who killed her brother many long years before. With this confession she hopes to save Sam from the legal action that would follow on an ex-convict's fall from grace. It was guilt and remorse over Sam's taking the blame for the killing that turned Henrietta into a pathetic alcoholic. Charles realizes that Henrietta and Sam still love each other, and refuses to press charges against Sam, declaring instead that he had been shot accidentally. Flusky in turn refuses to corroborate Henrietta's confession of murder, so the Fluskys go free. Charles goes back to Ireland and Sam and Henrietta find that their love has renewed itself and prepare for a happier future together.

REVIEWS

Howard Barnes in the New York Herald Tribune:

Alfred Hitchcock has tackled a difficult psychological theme in his new picture.... *Under Capricorn* has many of the great director's touches. Moreover, it has Ingrid Bergman doing her best acting in a long time, with Joseph Cotten and Michael Wilding supporting her valiantly. In tinted photography, it is a handsome period romance set in the Australia of 1831, but the basic material defeats a meticulous and artistic treatment. Conversation outweighs pictorial movement for most of two hours and there are only hints of the passion and melodrama on which this work might have blossomed.... As a

With Joseph Cotten

past master of melodrama [Hitchcock] has stumbled. It has taken all of Miss Bergman's nervous intensity, Cotten's suppressed violence, Miss Leighton's malignance, and Wilding's debonair intruding to keep *Under Capricorn* fluent and cumulative. . . . Hitchcock may be remembered for this piece of direction, but only for snatches of it.

Bosley Crowther in The New York Times:

With all due regard for the slyness of the mischief that rolls through this tale and for its touching potential of the misery with which it is heavily charged, it seems that neither Miss Bergman nor Mr. Hitchcock has tangled here with stuff of any better than penny-dreadful substance and superficial demands. As the beautiful Lady Henrietta who lives in the great Australian house with her beetle-browed ex-convict husband and quietly drowns herself in drink, Miss Bergman is called upon to put forth little more than some

With Michael Wilding

soggy displays of sozzled and sentimental maundering or of wide-eyed and dry-throated dread. The stuff for a solid characterization is simply not put her way. And Mr. Hitchcock, the director, has little more with which to stoke up steam than an unfolding tale of an ancient murder and an easily perceived villainess. . . . It is an overlong, overlabored essay on the torments of conscience and love which Mr. Hitchcock has beautifully filmed in Technicolor but painted in glaring blacks and whites.

Lawrence J. Quirk in Movies in Boston:

Under Capricorn is not Hitchcock at his best; I suspect the story is not really his cup of tea. But Miss Bergman is always interesting to watch, though she has in this instance been handed a role that is ill-defined and characterizationally murky.

In Newsweek:

While Hitchcock's Technicolor cameras colorfully recreate the lusty period, he succeeds in making the general narrative only intermittently suspenseful and compelling. Cotten is saddled with a role that is limited in both its appeal and its emotional range, and there are times when Miss Bergman finds the sad and sometimes tiresome Henrietta a little too much for even her recognized talent.

The Rossellini Period

Ingrid Bergman

Stromboli

RKO Radio, 1950

CAST

Ingrid Bergman, Mario Vitale, Renzo Cesana, Mario Sponza.

CREDITS

Produced and directed by Roberto Rossellini. Story by Signor Rossellini in collaboration with Art Cohn, Renzo Cesana, Sergio Amidei and G. P. Callegari. Camera: Otello Martelli. Music by Renzo Rossellini. Production assistant: Renzo Rossellini. Editor: Roland Gross. Running time, 89 minutes.

THE STORY

Karin *(Ingrid Bergman)*, a Czech refugee, seeks to escape from an Italian displaced persons' camp by marrying a young ex-soldier, Antonio *(Mario Vitale)*, who takes her back to his lonely island, Stromboli, in the Tyrrhenian Sea.

Secure in her new Italian citizenship, Karin tries to adjust to the primitive and drab life of the island, which is foreign to her passionate and life-loving nature. She attempts to make friends with the village women, who treat her suspiciously and hold aloof. She appeals at moments of doubt and bewilderment to the village priest *(Renzo Cesana)*, who offers only well-meant platitudes and likewise keeps her at a distance. She finds she has little in common with her taciturn young husband, who spends much of his time tuna-fishing. Only a young lighthouse keeper *(Mario Sponza)* offers the semblance of friendship.

Her husband considers her flighty, becomes irritated with her failure to conform to the local mores, and when he suspects her of dalliance with the lighthouse keeper he beats her and

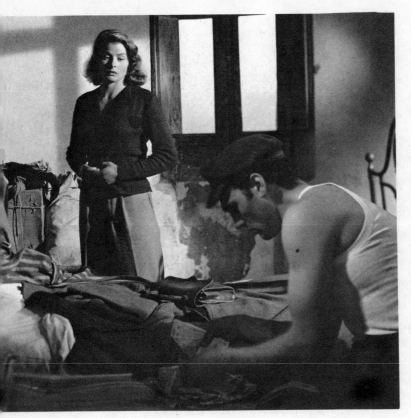

With Mario Vitale

nails boards to the windows and doors of their home, so as to imprison her. The realization that she is pregnant adds to Karin's bewilderment and depression. She enlists the aid of the lighthouse keeper in effecting her escape, and flees to the volcanic mountain of Stromboli, where she is caught in the acrid fumes of a lava flow. She falls asleep on the ground, and in the morning, after meditating and considering her course of action, she senses a kind of regeneration in herself and decides to return to the village and her husband and make what she can of her life there.

NOTE

The heavy Hollywood editing of this film reportedly destroyed its atmosphere and story coherence. Admittedly, there are plot ends left untied in the version as edited, and Rossellini's original concept is not realized. Earlier in the production phase, the film had been tentatively titled *After the Storm*.

REVIEWS

Lawrence J. Quirk in Movies in Boston:

Some of the intense criticism this film has encountered in the United States might well be due to the fact that Hollywood's production line has so accustomed us to slickly glib, lacquered cinema techniques that most of us do not take the time to reflect that unvarnished, realistic treatment can add considerable power to a film. Rossellini seems to have determined to rid Miss Bergman of certain acquired Hollywood mannerisms and those layers of California-style makeup that in some films made her look like an overpainted kewpie doll. Here she seems a down-to-earth, realistic type. The picture does have a grainy, true-to-life quality, and since Miss Bergman has always been an excellent actress despite the aforementioned heavy makeup and the ill-advised direction she sustained at times in Hollywood, she and the other cast members look real. The story could have happened easily in life. Rossellini complains that Hollywood editors butchered the film and deprived it of sense or meaning. Could be he's right and it should have been left alone. The insensitive editing by commercial-minded types, the fact that Americans are still not completely at home with Rossellini's cinematic innovations, and above all the puritanical American approach to the Rossellini-

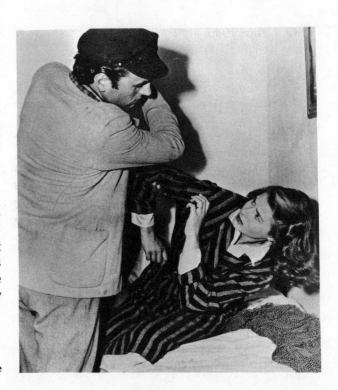

With Mario Vitale

With Mario Vitale

Bergman love affair—these seem to have conspired against a picture, which, as seen, may win no Oscars but isn't really all *that* bad! We expect the majority of critics cross-country to be against us in this evaluation, but we've said our say, like it or lump it!

A Studio Executive as quoted by Time:

It's a 20-minute travelogue of Stromboli in an 89-minute film. When things get dull, they throw in a little sex.

Bosley Crowther in The New York Times:

After all the unprecedented interest that [this film] has aroused—it being of course the fateful drama which Ingrid Bergman and Robert Rossellini have made—it comes as a startling anticlimax to discover that this widely heralded film is incredibly feeble, inarticulate, uninspiring and painfully banal. At least, the picture of this title that flashed upon screens here yesterday . . . cannot be more flatteringly described. Whether this dismal culmination of high hopes and distinguished enterprise can be blamed altogether on Rossellini, its producer-director, is not yet sure. Some share of the responsibility may be borne by its distributor, RKO. For, to add to the mystery and confusion already surrounding this film is the rumor that considerable re-editing was done in Hollywood by RKO upon the footage and the "cut" of the picture prepared by its producer-director in Italy, and a cable from Ros-

sellini, which arrived on Tuesday, implies that this is not the "version" originally arranged by him.

Otis L. Guernsey Jr. in the
New York Herald Tribune:

The much-discussed *Stromboli* is neither good Bergman, good Rossellini, nor good anything. Its theme might be defined as "be bored along with me" as it traces the passionless discomforts of a wife who cannot adjust herself to a primitive, unfamiliar community. There is no depth to Ingrid Bergman's performance, no vitality in Roberto Rossellini's direction. There is neither sense nor sensation to be found in it. . . . The human relationships are wan and shadowy in a continuity which is flat and confused. . . . *Stromboli* profits only from notoriety; as a film drama it is a waste of talent and a waste of time.

In Look:

An interesting experiment . . . filmed in the off-the-cuff realism Rossellini made famous in *Open City* and *Paisan*. Tells simple story of wife's rebellion against burdens of marriage. . . . Used untutored fishermen and villagers in leading roles and started out with no script. . . . [Rossellini] wrote the film with his camera day by day. . . . When the company went to Farfa to shoot the beginning of the picture, Rossellini found such interesting new characters that he revised and reshot an important opening scene.

Europa '51

(The Greatest Love)

I.F.E. Releasing Corp., 1951, 1954 (U.S. release)

CAST

Ingrid Bergman, Alexander Knox, Ettore Giannini, Giulietta Masina, Teresa Pellati, Sandro Franchina, William Tubbs, Alfred Browne.

CREDITS

Produced and directed by Roberto Rossellini. A Ponti-DeLaurentiis Production. Screenplay by Signor Rossellini, Sandro de Leo, Mario Pannunzio, Ivo Perilli and Brunello Rondi, from Signor Rossellini's original story. Running time, 118 minutes.

THE STORY

Irene Girard (Ingrid Bergman) and her husband George (Alexander Knox) are well-to-do Americans living in Rome. When her young son kills himself because of what he conceives to be his mother's neglectful attitude toward him,

Irene is consumed with guilt and remorse. To distract herself from her unhappiness, she goes into the streets of Rome, and without exhibiting either an organized or a sensibly conceived program of philanthropic good works, sets out to help everyone she meets, indiscriminately and without regard to the realities of the situation.

She helps wayward mothers, prostitutes, the dregs of the populace, in ways that are not always wise, and her bewildered husband and socially prominent family try to indulge her for a time, feeling that grief has affected her judgment—but when she helps the son of a pensioner, a young criminal, to escape the Italian police, her husband decides that she has crossed the line into mental illness, and she is confined to an institution.

The point is made that indiscriminate, "fool of

With Ettore Giannini

God"-style philanthropy, when not genuinely actuated by religious or political concepts, is regarded as eccentric and pathological, and that people everywhere find themselves uncomfortable with "do-gooders" who lack true direction or purpose. Among those to whom Irene tries to "do good" are Passerotto *(Giulietta Masina)*, an unmarried mother, and Ines *(Teresa Pellati)*, an irredeemable prostitute who finally dies.

REVIEWS

Otis L. Guernsey, Jr. in the
New York Herald Tribune (1954):

Once again Miss Bergman is playing a woman exalted beyond ordinary measure as her tears of grief turn to tears of sympathy. She is statuesque in the part—the marble cracks occasionally, but its lines are severe and other-worldly. Her per-

With Alexander Knox

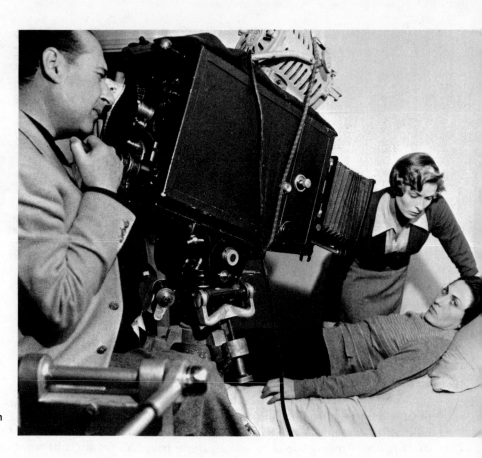

Rossellini directing Miss Bergman
and Teresa Pellati

formance is one of almost monotonous perfection. She is wrenched from the ranks of humanity by the death of her child, and she is never quite seen clearly or intimately as a human being again. Rossellini has striven mightily to do something important in this film, which is based on an idea of his own. He has tried to capture an element of saintliness and demonstrate that modern society would find it difficult to tolerate this quality. But his movie is at its best when its feet are most firmly planted on the ground, beside the pathetic deathbed of a prostitute, in the heavy, harsh atmosphere of a factory, or in the furtive closeups of sanatorium inmates. There are faint echoes of *The Miracle* in the connection between universal love and insanity in *The Greatest Love,* but they are heavily muffled in outward decorum and evident high purpose. Some of the details are grainy and poignant.

Bosley Crowther in The New York Times (1954):

The transfer of Ingrid Bergman to the realm of Italian films has obviously not resulted in an advancement in her acting career. . . . The fault is quite plainly not Miss Bergman's in this dismal and dolorous account of the frustrations of a socially distinguished young matron in finding an outlet for her urge to do good. She does what she's asked to do fitly, with a maximum of confusion and dismay revealed in her lovely eyes and features as she represents her thwarted woman's grief. And it is notable that Miss Bergman has grown older gracefully, with more strength and matronly beauty in her eternally interesting face.

Lawrence J. Quirk in Screen Slants (retrospective review):

It may well happen—say about 1975—that the Rossellini-Bergman films of the early 1950s will be appreciated more than they were at the time of their original release. They were not flawless, but they did possess a grainy sincerity and a let-the-chips-fall-where-they-may individuality that dared to fail—and did, at least in that period—but perhaps they were *ahead* of the period. Certainly they had clearer statements to make than some of the photographically tricked-up but thematically pointless European films of the sixties touted by young longhairs whose enthusiasm typically outdistances their judgment.

We, The Women

(Siamo Donne)

Titanus, 1953

CAST

Ingrid Bergman, Anna Magnani, Isa Miranda, Alida Valli, Emma Danieli, Anna Amendola.

CREDITS

"The Chicken," third of five segments in this episodic film, starred Miss Bergman and was directed by Roberto Rossellini. The stories and screenplays were by Cesare Zavattini. Luigi Chiarini collaborated on the screenplay of "The Chicken" and Otello Martelli photographed.

Each of the five segments ran roughly one-half hour.

Episode I, which starred Emma Danieli and Anna Amendola, was directed by Alfredo Guarini and photographed by Domenico Scala. Episode II, which starred Alida Valli, was directed by Gianni Francioli and photographed by Enzo Serafin. Luigi Chiarini collaborated on the screenplay. Episode IV, which followed the Bergman-Rossellini segment, starred Isa Miranda, was directed by Luigi Zampa and photographed by Domenico Scala. Luigi Chiarini and Georgio Prosperi collaborated on the screenplay. Episode V

starred Anna Magnani, was directed by Luchino Visconti and photographed by Gabor Pogany. Suso Cecchi D'Amico collaborated on the screenplay. Music was by Alessandro Cicognini. Alfredo Guarini supervised production.

THE STORY

The five episodes gave insights into problems, major and minor, of a cross-section of actresses. Signor Zavattini's stories were reportedly based on actual occurrences. We see actresses weathering disappointment in competition for roles, fighting rivals in the romance ratrace, fussing over pets and torn between family and career. The Rossellini-Bergman segment had to do with a lady (Miss Bergman) who has grown some beautiful roses, which she highly prizes. A recalcitrant chicken finds the roses enticing, but for a different reason: he wants to eat them. A contest develops between the actress's visual enthrallment with her rose garden, which she has tended with meticulous care, and the chicken's hunger for the inviting petals all around him. The serio comic proceedings find the lady

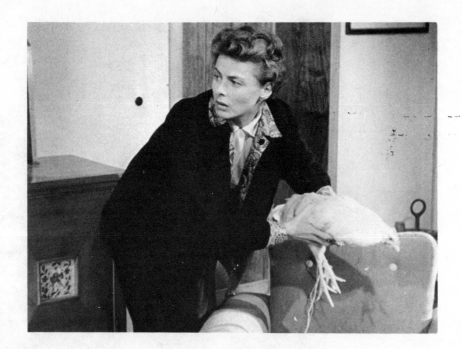

and the fowl attempting to outwit each other in the interests of their separate, and quite disparate, aims. The chicken gets to gobble some roses, but the actress gets in her licks, too.

REVIEWS

Lawrence J. Quirk in Current Screen:

This Rossellini-Bergman segment is certainly lighter than their usual vein, subject-wise. Seen at a private showing, the film is composed of five quite disparate segments starring such luminaries of the Italian cinema as Alida Valli, Anna Magnani and Isa Miranda, all of whom get themselves into variegated situations tailored to the individual actress' cinematic personality. Miss Bergman, directed by her husband, drew a rather felicitous assignment and situation, if only because it permits her to vary her pace by indulging her humorous side. Highly visual, and serio-comic, the proceedings will never rival the didoes of Chaplin, Lloyd or even Joan Davis (not Bette, Joan, and we don't mean Joan *Crawford* either!) and the shades of such clowns as Zasu Pitts and Judy Canova and Martha Raye can rest easy. But Miss Bergman, not exactly a stranger to comedic dalliance, manages to inject some excitement into the goings-on and the brief running time of the segment (called "The Chicken") permits her to put on more or less of a one-woman show (with the chicken as co-star). However, since *she* can talk, and *he* can only cluck,

Miss Bergman has the advantage of the fowl— in more ways than one, it turns out.

In Film Di Questi Giorni: (Italian) (1953):

Miss Bergman offers a sympathetically ironic study of fussy self-concern . . . as the actress who is worried about the chicken's threat to her rose garden. . . . She also demonstrates here that she possesses a quietly-effective streak of realistic comic spirit.

Journey to Italy

(Viaggio in Italia)

Titanus, 1954

CAST

Ingrid Bergman, George Sanders, Paul Muller, Anna Proclemer, Maria Mauban, Leslie Daniels, Natalia Rai, Jackie Frost.

CREDITS

Titanus release of a Roberto Rossellini Production in association with Sveva-Junior Films. Directed by Roberto Rossellini. Story and screenplay by Signor Rossellini and Vitaliano Brancati. Music by Renzo Rossellini. Cameraman: Enro Sarafin. Film editor: Jolanda Bonvenuti. Premiered in Rome, October 19, 1954. Running time, 100 minutes.

NOTE

An English version (80 minutes) was shown in New York under the title Strangers in 1955; the film is also known as A Trip to Italy. During shooting, Rossellini fiddled with a number of tentative titles, among them New Wine and Such Is My Love, the latter a George Sanders suggestion that Rossellini rejected as being too sentimental.

THE STORY

Alexander Joyce (George Sanders), a London business executive, and his wife Katherine (Ingrid Bergman) find that their ten-year marriage has become a bore, and that they are drawing further and further apart. At this point, they learn that they have inherited a house in Italy. They decide to travel to Naples to inspect the house and get a change from the routine of their English life. The Italian climate and human atmosphere affect them deeply, and their habits and emotional conditionings are altered subtly. Close to divorce in England, they almost decide to go through with a complete marital severance in their new surroundings. Alexander dallies briefly with a prostitute (Anna Proclemer) and Katherine's un-

With George Sanders

happiness and sense of rootlessness grow. But there is still an underlying attachment for each other, and it revives full-force during a religious festival which they both attend. Alexander and Katherine finally realize that there is still much worth salvaging in their marriage and they decide to try again, on a firmer footing.

REVIEWS

Whit. in Variety:

Dull and plodding fare, [the picture] will have little appeal [in America]. . . . Rossellini achieves a feeling of reality in the relationship of the couple but otherwise his direction shows little distinction and he's faced with hackneyed dialogue badly dubbed. Lensed partly in Naples, some of the street scenes are interesting, but these are only flashes. Spectator must wait for the femme star, for no apparent reason, to wander through four museums and ruins, which tends to slow even the meandering pace previously established. . . . Sanders is suavely restrained and Miss Bergman, although poorly photographed, nonetheless lends charm to an indefinite role.

Lawrence J. Quirk in Current Screen:

Ingrid Bergman and George Sanders, last seen together in *Rage in Heaven* in 1941, find themselves here in a less-than-heavenly marital alliance which has reached the breaking point. . . . Roberto Rossellini tries hard to instill conviction into the proceedings but it all seems pointless and dull. . . . Miss Bergman, of course, lends her own special distinction to anything in which she appears. . . . There are extraneous scenes which lend some Rossellini-style atmospheric interest to the picture, but they do nothing to advance the story. . . . Chalk it up as another miss for the Rossellinis.

In Films in Review:

Poorly written, incompetently directed, atrociously edited.

Joan at the Stake

(Giovanna D'Arco al Rogo)

ENIC, 1954

CAST

Ingrid Bergman, Tullio Carminati, Giacinto Prantelli, Augusto Romani, Plinio Clabassi, Saturno Meletti, Agnese Dubbini, Pietro de Palma, Aldo Tenossi. Voices of: Pina Esca, Marcella Pillo, Giovanni Acolati, Miriam Pirazzini.

CREDITS

Directed by Roberto Rossellini. Screenplay by Roberto Rossellini, based on the story and dialogue of Paul Claudel and on the oratorio of Paul Claudel and Arthur Honegger in which

Signor Rossellini presented Miss Bergman in Paris, London, Stockholm, Barcelona, etc. (Miss Bergman's role was non-singing).

THE STORY

Miss Bergman speaks the part of Joan throughout the filmization of the oratorio with which she and Mr. Rossellini had toured throughout Europe. The story follows Joan of Arc's career from her initial visions through her death by burning at the stake. As noted in the section on

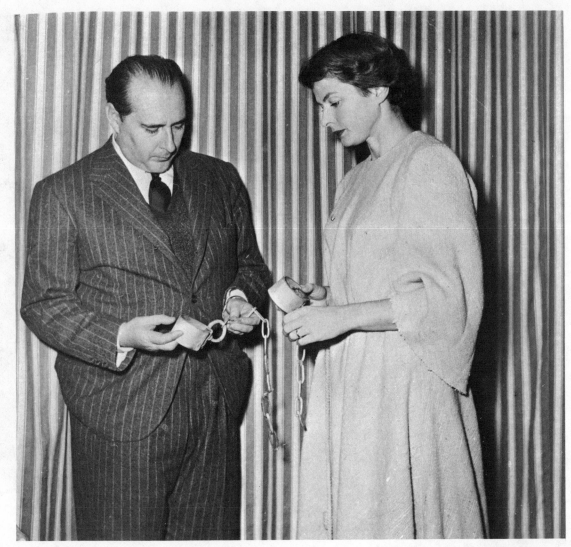

With Roberto Rossellini on the set

the stage version elsewhere, the piece is a blending of choral singing, spoken drama and crowd scenes, with many supernumeraries on hand.

NOTE

Rossellini had great difficulty in getting the film sold or even booked into theatres. Those who saw the film thought it insufficiently cinematic and rather a static and literal film transcription of the live performance.

REVIEWS

Lawrence J. Quirk in Current Screen:

Whatever its merits judged strictly as a motion picture, it is only right and fair that future students of both Miss Bergman's and Mr. Rossellini's work should have a record of this oratorio in which they toured Europe valiantly at what perhaps was the lowest period, morale-wise and financially, of both their careers.

Ingrid Bergman (as quoted by Joseph Henry Steele):

No one wants to invest money in it because it is opera. But we are stubborn and will do it anyway. We love it and believe in it. You just have to do things that way; not what other people think you should do. If you make a mistake, that's too bad. But surely, that is the only way to live.

Fear
(Angst)

Minerva Films, 1955

CAST

Ingrid Bergman, Mathias Wiemann, Renate Mannhardt, Kurt Kreuger, Elise Aulinger.

CREDITS

A Minerva Films Production. Directed by Roberto Rossellini in Germany. Screenplay by Roberto Rossellini, Sergio Amidei and Franz Graf Treuberg. Based on the novel Der Angst *by Stefan Zweig. Music by Renzo Rossellini. Cameraman: Peter Heller. Photographed in 1954. Shown in Italy and elsewhere in 1955. Running time, 91 minutes.*

THE STORY

The restless, love-hungry wife *(Ingrid Bergman)* of a wealthy factory owner *(Mathias Wiemann)* who is somewhat older, has taken a lover *(Kurt Kreuger),* though she still feels a sincere if non-romantic affection for her husband. She has settled down to a two-timing *modus vivendi* which she finds tolerably satisfying and imagines she has been discreet about it. But the lover's former paramour *(Renate Mannhardt)* takes advantage of the wife's involvement, and subjects her to diabolical blackmail pressures. Fearful of a scandal, and anxious to hang on to her marriage, the wife pays large sums to the blackmailer. Then she discovers that her own husband has instigated the blackmailing, using the lover's ex-flame as a front. Caught in an emotional impasse that she regards as humiliating and intolerable, the wife considers suicide, but is rescued from it by her husband. Both realize that they have erred, and they are reconciled.

REVIEWS

Angelo Solmi in Oggi (Italian):

[Miss Bergman and Mr. Rossellini] will either have to change their style of work radically—or retire into dignified silence. The abyss into which

With Kurt Kreuger

With Mathias Wiemann

Bergman and Rossellini have plunged can be measured by *Angst*. This is not because this film is any worse than their other recent motion pictures together, but because after half-a-dozen tries with negative results it proves the inability of the couple to create anything acceptable to the public or the critics. Once the world's unquestioned Number One [film] star and successor to Greta Garbo, Miss Bergman in her latest pictures has been only a shadow of herself.

Lawrence J. Quirk in Current Screen:

Undeterred by some consistently harsh criticisms of their screen efforts since *Stromboli*, Miss Bergman and Mr. Rossellini have come up again with a well-intentioned effort in this melodramatic story, shot in Germany, of a wife who submits to blackmail rather than let her husband know of her adulterous affair. Mr. Rossellini gives the treatment some original touches, and Miss Bergman is intense and sincere. The picture is no award-winner, either by European or American standards, but there is just enough earnest work in it to leave the impression that, if they keep on going, the Rossellinis may yet have the detractors of their screen work eating crow. This

time around, they get a healthy B-plus for effort, and an A for gutsy persistence.

Hans. in Variety:

The first German Ingrid Bergman film after sixteen years turns out to be slightly disappointing. Except for the outstanding performance given by Miss Bergman, there is nothing new or particularly exciting about this one. In transferring Stefan Zweig's novel to the modern era, the plot loses its conviction and dramatic grip. As a result, *Fear* lacks the necessary suspense. Name of Miss Bergman may lure many patrons here and probably outside this country. The Swedish actress has not lost her natural charm and beauty. . . . Had it not been for Miss Bergman in the femme lead, the picture might have become a total flop. The few other players are considerably overshadowed by her. That also applies to Mathias Wiemann, who portrays Ingrid Bergman's husband with noblesse. *Fear* gives evidence of the artistic decline of one of the well-known post-war directors, Roberto Rossellini. In this German opus, he lacks style and roundness, and there are comparatively few scenes which have the Rossellini touch.

144

The Renaissance

Anastasia

20th Century-Fox, 1956

CAST

Ingrid Bergman, Yul Brynner, Helen Hayes, Akim Tamiroff, Martita Hunt, Felix Aylmer, Sacha Piteoff, Ivan Desny, Natalie Schafer, Gregoire Gromoff, Karel Stepanek, Ina De La Haye, Katherine Kath.

CREDITS

Produced by Buddy Adler. Directed by Anatole Litvak. Screenplay by Arthur Laurents from a play by Marcel Maurette as adapted by Guy Bolton. Director of photography: Jack Hildyard. Music by Alfred Newman. Art direction: Andrei Andrejew and Bill Andrews. Costumes: Rene Hubert. Music orchestrations: Edward B. Powell. Russian music arranged by Michel Michelet. Set decorations by Andrew Low. Assistant director: Gerry O'Hara. Film editor: Bert Bates. Hair styles: Johnnie Johnson. Makeup: Dave Aylott. Deluxe Color and CinemaScope. Running time, 105 minutes.

NOTE

For her performance in this film, Miss Bergman received her second Academy Award.

THE STORY

Bounine (Yul Brynner), a White Russian general, and his fellow schemers who are with him in exile in the 1920s, encounter an unknown woman (Ingrid Bergman), who has been found wandering half-mad, physically depleted, and suffering from amnesia. She bears a strong resemblance to the Grand Duchess Anastasia, daughter of Nicholas II, last Czar of Russia, who was presumably murdered with the rest of the Imperial Family in 1918. There have been rumors between 1918 and 1928 throughout Europe to the effect that Anastasia was the only one of the family to survive the mass shooting in the cellar at Ekaterinburg. Bounine and his friends decide to groom and train The Unknown and try to pass

her off as Anastasia. If successful, they hope to share in the fortune which would be hers if rumors that Nicholas II had deposited large funds outside Russia should prove correct.

Bounine coaches The Unknown relentlessly in matters of Imperial etiquette. He drills her in a host of details and facts relating to Anastasia. The hitherto listless and vague girl begins to come to life and to assume a distinctive person-

ality. Bounine confronts her with former members of the Imperial court, and when she shows surprising flashes of knowledge and insight into the life of the original Anastasia, Bounine is surprised. A skeptical old court chamberlain of the Romanov court *(Felix Aylmer)* at first turns from the claimant in scorn when Bounine forces a meeting; then even he is converted when The Unknown suddenly assumes an aura that only a

With Yul Brynner

148

With Yul Brynner

person of the highest station could project authentically. More and more the true personality of The Unknown emerges, and she recalls facts about her former life that only the Grand Duchess could have known. Bounine is driven to wonder if he does not, after all, have the authentic article on his hands. But a final test is necessary—and it is one that "Anastasia" must pass.

Bounine takes her to Copenhagen to meet the Dowager Empress Marie, her grandmother, who, after many disappointments at the hands of claimants and pretenders, refuses to see her. Through the good offices of Prince Paul *(Ivan Desny)* and the Baroness Von Livenbaum *(Martita Hunt)* the claimant, whom the Empress has covertly observed from a distance at the theatre, finally gains access to the Presence. When she

reveals personal traits (a cough that she develops when excited) that only her grandmother could recognize, the old Empress joyfully accepts her as the authentic Grand Duchess Anastasia and takes her into her home.

Bounine has gradually fallen in love with Anastasia, as he admits to the Empress, but his crude, taciturn personality makes it difficult for him to confess his feelings. Anastasia has become engaged to Prince Paul, but when the Empress asks Anastasia if she loves Paul, she replies that she merely "likes" him. She has herself fallen in love with Bounine, and the Empress, aware now of their mutual feeling, so arranges it that when faced with a life of exalted but lonely station or happiness with Bounine, Anastasia is permitted to choose the latter.

149

With Helen Hayes

As the pitiful and destitute stranger who is championed as the last surviving member of the presumably massacred Russian Imperial family, she is eloquent and moving and richly resourceful in her delineation of the half-maddened woman's emotional meanderings and inner confusions. . . . Miss Helen Hayes, great lady of the American theatre, is utterly impressive as the Dowager Empress of Russia, a lonely but proud old lady who lives in her Copenhagen castle with forlorn memories of a happier day, and who had been rendered bitter and suspicious by the succession of fake claimants to Anastasia's title. Miss Hayes and Miss Bergman are both superb in the film's climactic scene, famous in the annals of the stage, where the play had a long run. Here Miss Bergman attempts to convince Miss Hayes that she is truly her grand-daughter. The wonderful emotional counterpoint, the cross-currents of feeling, with the old lady struggling between unbelief and a wistful desire to accept the forlorn girl; the younger woman pitifully desirous of a recognition that will spell a personal identity and reunion with her loved ones, has to be seen to be appreciated. Miss Bergman, here and throughout the film, establishes her claim to Academy Award nominee status for 1956.

With Helen Hayes

REVIEWS

Lawrence J. Quirk in Motion Picture Herald:

Anastasia is grand-manner film-making. This means that it is in the great tradition of the lavish production budget, the top-drawer cast, the fascinating dramatic story told with elan and amidst impressive settings. And with the magic of CinemaScope and color by Deluxe, the sure, seasoned direction of Anatole Litvak and the shrewd producing instinct of Buddy Adler, a film of this type cannot fail. As the starring centerpieces in this masterfully constructed cinematic tour-de-force, Ingrid Bergman, Yul Brynner and Helen Hayes offer a battery of star-power that is likewise in the tradition of the days of yore. The film was photographed in Paris, London and Copenhagen. Miss Bergman, who returns to the American screen after a seven-year absence, during which she made films for European companies, demonstrates an impressive growth in her art since the days when she had a widespread and devoted American following. At 41, she is at the peak of her acting accomplishment.

With Sacha Piteoff and Yul Brynner

Bosley Crowther in The New York Times:

[The film] has gained pictorial scope and emotional dimensions in reaching the cinematic form. For Mr. Laurents has wisely given it geographical ranges, added strong scenes that the play barely suggested and expanded the conflicts within the heroine. Anatole Litvak has smartly staged it for a fine projection of its human ironies. And it is played with keen sensitivity by Ingrid Bergman, Yul Brynner and Helen Hayes. Miss Bergman's performance is nothing short of superb as she traces the progress of a woman from the depths of derangement and despair through a struggle with doubt and disillusion to the accomplishment of courage, pride and love. It is a beautifully molded performance, worthy of an Academy Award, and particularly gratifying in the light of Miss Bergman's long absence from commercial films.

Hollis Alpert in Saturday Review:

. . . A theatrically effective play has been turned into an entertaining, if rather theatrical, movie,

in which the acting is pretty topnotch. . . . The picture marks the return of Ingrid Bergman to the American screen. . . . Whether by accident or design, Mr. Litvak has given the film a coldly handsome mounting, a tired sort of elegance. . . . Miss Bergman is given the chance to run a gamut —from the haggard, dispirited woman who has lost hold of her identity to the regal creature who convinces her compatriots that she is the Grand Duchess, daughter of the late Czar of all the Russias. The premises throughout may be sentimental, but Miss Bergman is the real thing.

William K. Zinsser in the
New York Herald Tribune:

Miss Bergman is still a very beautiful woman. Her face has a new maturity and a hint of fatigue, which suit her well in this role. She begins as a broken, helpless girl searching with vacant eyes for some glimmer of the past. Gradually she becomes a radiant woman who dresses and moves with the instinctive grace of royalty.

With Jean Marais and Juliette Greco

Paris Does Strange Things

Warner Brothers, 1957

CAST

Ingrid Bergman, Mel Ferrer, Jean Marais, Juliette Greco, Marjane, George Higgins, J. Richard.

CREDITS

A Jean Renoir Production released by Warner Brothers. Directed by Jean Renoir. Screenplay by Jean Renoir, based on his original story. Color by Technicolor. Cameraman: Claude Renoir. Music by Joseph Kosma. Film editor: Borys Lewin. Running time, 86 minutes.

THE STORY

Elena *(Ingrid Bergman)*, a beautiful but impoverished Polish princess, goes adventuring in the frivolous Paris of the 1880s. Giddy, ironic and flirtatious in her attitude toward men, Elena enjoys being a sort of "power" behind whatever "thrones" pop up, and tends to gravitate toward men who she imagines "need" her in the direction of their lives and careers. Once these men become successful, she loses interest and drops them.

Her current target is an important French general, Rolan *(Jean Marais)*, whose political career Elena wants to help promote. She becomes involved in a rather elaborate and unrealistic plot to persuade the popular Rolan to take over the French government via a coup d'état. The general blows hot and cold on the project, but Elena shores up his determination by such affectations as presenting him with lucky daisies and pep-talking and romancing him.

Dancing attendance on Elena is young Count Henri *(Mel Ferrer)*, who helps or hinders Elena in her projects depending on whatever mood he happens to be in. There is a wealth of assorted intrigues, both of the political and boudoir type, and Elena's silly machinations almost wreck the general's career before Henri finally succeeds in persuading her that it is time to forget "king-making" and political and social intrigue, and settle down with him. In time, Elena sees the shallowness of her life, realizes that her approach to men has been essentially superficial and self-centered, and gladly accepts the romantic advances of Henri.

With Mel Ferrer

NOTE

There was much criticism of the vagueness and obscurity of the film's story-line, which was not helped by injudicious cutting, in the misguided belief that it would make this Jean Renoir farce more palatable to American audiences. The net product emerged as neither fish, fowl nor good red herring plot-wise, and the English dubbing of the French dialogue film was also criticized. Among the film's various titles before release: *Elena and the Men, The Night Does Strange Things*.

With Jean Marais and Mel Ferrer

REVIEWS

Norman Cecil in Films in Review:

This French film is so bad it is noticed here solely in order to warn off anyone who might be seduced by the fact that Jean Renoir directed it. I suspect Renoir must have been trying to please both left and right simultaneously. In France, at the moment, such a feat is possible, in certain circles. But in this English-dubbed version nothing makes any sense whatever. Least of all Ingrid Bergman (had she been re-introduced to the U.S. in this film instead of in *Anastasia* her American career would have been over). . . . As for the story, I can only hope the French dialogue gave it a *soupçon* of sense.

*William K. Zinsser in the
New York Herald Tribune:*

Nothing can explain why [Miss Bergman] agreed to take the role, how the great Jean Renoir could have made such a picture, or why, having made it, he didn't throw it into the Seine. It is so bad that you may think he made it that way intentionally, on a dare. The plot is one of those turn-of-the-century affairs about wily ministers and scheming ladies in Paris. It's hard to say what they are all doing. . . . Miss Bergman is charming and beautiful and she deserves everybody's sympathy this morning.

Bosley Crowther in The New York Times:

Never was a film more aptly titled than *Paris Does Strange Things*. Everything about it is bewildering, from the utter obscurity of the script to the presence of Ingrid Bergman, Mel Ferrer, and Jean Marais as stars. And the fact that Jean Renoir was the director is the ultimate oddity. How this fiasco could have happened is difficult to explain. The kindest supposition is that Warners, which is releasing it here, tried to improve it with cutting and only made it worse. If ever there was a trace of clarity in its story of a Polish princess taking part in a nineteenth century intrigue to pull a coup d'état in France, it is lost in the mishmash of footage. Believe us, it doesn't make sense, despite the fact that it is fitted with English dialogue. . . . It appears that M. Renoir was undecided whether this was a romantic drama or a slapstick farce, so the actors gave it to him both ways, indiscriminately and at the top of their lungs. Miss Bergman, in rather striking costumes, is like a chicken with its head cut off. She simply flings her arms wildly and bumps

With Mel Ferrer

into people. Toward the end she grows tired and gives up. The one clue to why this strange concoction was hastily booked at the Paramount is that Miss Bergman just won an "Oscar." She should use it to hit somebody over the head.

Jesse Zunser in Cue:

Its jigsaw non sequiturs and squirreling confusions in plot, characterization and editing, its grubbed writing and disordered direction simply defy description in limited space. . . . The plot crudities and confusions are matched by the fumbling of the unhappy players trapped in this elaborate film farrago.

Fred Hift in Variety:

Considering the tradition of quality that attaches to the name of Jean Renoir, [the picture] comes as something of a shock. It is a silly, pointless little satire that outstays its welcome after the first half-hour and becomes an outright bore before it's over. . . . Miss Bergman retains her appealing dignity.

With Cary Grant

Indiscreet

Warner Brothers, 1958

CAST

Cary Grant, Ingrid Bergman, Cecil Parker, Phyllis Calvert, David Kossoff, Megs Jenkins, Oliver Johnston, Middleton Woods.

CREDITS

Produced and directed by Stanley Donen. A Grandon production. Screenplay by Norman Krasna, based on his play, Kind Sir. Art director: Don Ashton. Color photography: Frederick A. Young. Cameraman: Robert Walker. Music by Richard Bennett and Ken Jones, conducted by Muir Mathieson. Song "Indiscreet" by Sammy Cahn and James Van Heusen. Associate producer: Sidney Streeter. Film editor: Jack Harris. Filmed in London. Color by Technicolor. Running time, 100 minutes.

THE STORY

Ann Kalman (Ingrid Bergman) is a world-famous and wealthy actress who lives in a luxurious apartment in London, near Buckingham Palace. Through her sister and brother-in-law (Phyllis Calvert and Cecil Parker) Ann meets confirmed bachelor Philip Adams (Cary Grant), an American wizard of finance who is in London for a NATO dinner. Philip makes it a policy to protect his single status by pretending to all likely females that he is trammeled with a wife who refuses to give him a divorce.

He gives Ann this same line, and she believes him. Happily, they embark on an affair, but soon Philip is forced to return to America. He plans to surprise her on her birthday with a sudden and unexpected visit via plane, but Ann gets the

With Cecil Parker

With Megs Jenkins

same idea and plans to surprise *him* by flying to the United States. However, her sister tips her off that Philip is not married, and Ann in a rage cries, "How dare he make love to me when he isn't a married man!" (the film's most famous and oft-mentioned comedy line).

Ann then decides to play Philip's game and punish him by producing an ex-suitor in her apartment at the point of Philip's return, to make it look as if she is two-timing him. But the ex-suitor is toted off for an emergency appendectomy, and to carry out the boudoir ruse, Ann is forced to resort to her hapless chauffeur, Carl *(David Kossoff)*. Philip arrives with word that his "wife" has agreed to give him a divorce. Ann's "lover" then makes his appearance and Philip, humiliated and angered, stalks out of the apartment. He returns later to inform Ann that he must have been out of his mind to consider marrying her. At this point, he discovers the hoax—and proposes marriage.

REVIEWS

In Time:

[The film] in the Broadway version (*Kind Sir*)

With Megs Jenkins

156

With Cary Grant

Paul V. Beckley in the New York Herald Tribune:

The presence of both Ingrid Bergman and Cary Grant in a romantic comedy ought to guarantee enough charm to raise a lot of expectations; it is pleasant to report that in *Indiscreet* this pair cavort in such a debonair style that none of those expectations is in serious danger of disappointment. Furthermore, the comedy is . . . never serious nor dawdling, and can be safely recommended to those of relatively stringent taste. . . . The success [of the film] owes much to the sharp direction of Stanley Donen, but it is the marvelously flexible acting of Miss Bergman that gives it much of its subtle articulateness. There are sequences in which the changing facial expressions of Miss Bergman and Grant carry the situation forward with scarcely any dialogue to assist. With such facile performances, dialogue would at times be almost an intrusion.

was the sort of romantic comedy that is all dressed up but obviously has no place to go—but then, Broadway scarcely has the resources that are required to gild this sort of lulu. Instead of $100,000, the movie's producer-director Stanley Donen had about $1,500,000 to squander. Instead of painted flats, he had the city of London for his backdrop, and some of the city's stateliest halls for his interiors. Instead of nature's timid hues, he had Technicolor. Instead of a couple of merely famous names—Mary Martin and Charles Boyer—he had two of the biggest that have ever been in the business—Ingrid Bergman and Cary Grant. . . . *Indiscreet* is a conventional comedy of what Hollywood supposes to be upper-class manners, but it is flicked off in the high old style of hilarity that U.S. moviemakers seem to have forgotten in recent years. Director Donen deserves a cash-register-ringing cheer. Actress Bergman, always lovely to look at, is thoroughly competent in the first comedy role that she has played for Hollywood. And Cary Grant is in a class by himself when it comes to giving a girl a yacht.

In Films in Review:

Much more entertaining (than the play) due to the presence of Cary Grant and Ingrid Bergman in beautiful clothes and settings. Please don't start thinking about *Indiscreet* after you've enjoyed it. *Indiscreet* is froufrou that won't bear examination and is none the worse for that.

With Cary Grant

A. H. Weiler in The New York Times:

Miss Bergman, as the lady in love, emerges as a most charming comedienne, a professional who can handle a gaily irreverent line of dialogue as easily as a dramatic declaration. . . . *Indiscreet* is as light, airy and weightless as a soufflé. But all concerned have made it a most palatable concoction.

The Inn of the Sixth Happiness

20th Century-Fox, 1958

CAST

Ingrid Bergman, Curt Jurgens, Robert Donat, Michael David, Athene Seyler, Ronald Squire, Moultrie Kelsall, Richard Wattis, Peter Chong, Teai Chin, Edith Sharpe, Joan Young, Lian-Shin Yang, Noel Hood, Burt Kwouk.

CREDITS

Produced by Buddy Adler. Directed by Mark Robson. Screenplay by Isobel Lennart, based on the novel The Small Woman, by Alan Burgess. Director of photography: Frederick A. Young. Cameraman: Robert Walker. Costumes by Margaret Furse. Art directors: John Box and Geoffrey Drake. Music by Malcolm Arnold. Orchestra conducted by Malcolm Arnold. Production supervisor: James Newcom. Film editor: Ernest Walter.

Produced in CinemaScope and Technicolor. Running time, 157 minutes.

THE STORY

Gladys Aylward (Ingrid Bergman), a London domestic in the service of a retired explorer, Sir Francis (Ronald Squire), is briefed by her employer on conditions in China. Sir Francis tells Gladys about an English missionary, Sara Lanson (Athene Seyler), who has set up a hostelry in the mountains of North China. Here she takes in transient mule drivers, provides them with food and lodging, and tries by subtle means to convert them to Christianity. Gladys decides that she will join Miss Lanson in her work.

Her application for missionary work is re-

With Robert Donat and Curt Jurgens

jected because of her lack of formal education, but she saves enough money to travel to China via the Trans-Siberian Railway. Eventually she reaches the inn and Miss Lanson, and becomes her aide.

Gradually, she wins over the people of the area, with her good works and humble, friendly approach. Soon she is known as "Jan-Ai" (The One Who Loves People). After Miss Lanson's death, Gladys goes to work as a foot inspector (to enforce a government edict against binding of females' feet) at the behest of a tired and cynical mandarin *(Robert Donat)*, who is irritated by her meddling and sends her on foot-inspection trips to get rid of her. But upon her return from an arduous trip, he finds himself respectful of her dedication and courage and becomes her friend.

Captain Lin Nan *(Curt Jurgens)*, a Chinese Army officer, comes into the district to enforce discipline in the face of the impending Japanese 1931 invasion. Gladys meanwhile has succeeded in quelling a prison riot with her healing presence, and when Lin Nan finds it necessary to warn the people of the countryside against the Japanese, Gladys, through bandits she has befriended and who are now devoted to her, manages to aid him in his efforts. Lin Nan and Gladys

gradually fall in love, and before he leaves to rejoin the Chinese forces, he gives her a jade ring as a token of his feeling, and promises that they will someday be permanently together.

The Japanese attack, and it becomes necessary to march 100 motherless children to a mission safe in the interior. Before Gladys volunteers for, and leaves on, the mission with the children, the Mandarin offers her a parting gift: his conversion to Christianity.

Gladys and the children struggle many miles across rugged Chinese terrain to the village where the mission is located. Here they are greeted with cheers by the villagers, who have heard of Gladys' problems in transporting the children there against almost overwhelming odds. As she arrives, with the children, in the midst of the cheering people, she confronts the very man who had first declared her unfit for missionary work. He greets her humbly and warmly, and offers the protection of the mission. Gladys leaves the children there, and looking at the jade ring, declares that her life lies back from whence she came, and that she must return.

REVIEWS

Frank Leyendecker in Boxoffice:

It is Miss Bergman's glowing portrayal of an

159

With Curt Jurgens

obscure Englishwoman with little formal education but with the inner drive to dedicate her life to the downtrodden people of China that gives the picture the meaning and force to make it a cinematic achievement.

In Time:

[The film] has just about everything the mass public is said to want. It has Ingrid Bergman in a part so flagrantly sympathetic that Hollywood may not dare refuse her a third Oscar. It has Curt Jurgens, a German matinee idol who looks like John Wayne with a monocle scar, and it has the late Robert Donat, playing a sort of Chinese Mr. Chips in his most magniloquent style. . . . It has CinemaScope, De Luxe color, 2,000 Chinese ex-

With Robert Donat

tras, a $5,000,000 budget, a $450,000 set, a running time of 157 minutes—without an intermission. It has love, war, religion, riot, murder, spectacle, horror, comedy, music, dancing, miscegenation, cops, robbers, concubines, children, horses, the best scenery in Wales, the worst *chinoiserie* ever seen on screen, a success story that is invincibly feminist and relentlessly cheery, and more sheer treacle than anybody has seen since the Great Boston Molasses Flood (1919). The film is said to be based on the life of Gladys Aylward, an English missionary. But somehow, as tricked up and blooped out to fill the Cinema-Scope screen, the woman's simple story comes to seem rather like a Cecil B. DeMille version of "Now I Lay Me Down to Sleep." . . . The pity is that in itself the story is strongly moving. The sacrifice of self for the sake of others is surely one of the profoundest experiences that human beings have attained, and it is not often that this experience has been so sharply dramatized as it is in the life of Gladys Aylward. Something of the woman's flame-simple, stone-actual spirit is unquestionably preserved in the film, but all too often the religious force of her example is prettily dissipated in the delusive grandeur of the wide screen, and safely explained away in entertainingly heroic tropes and grossly commercial moments of the heart.

In the New York Herald Tribune:

. . . Essentially a movie of heart. It has one of the year's warmest performances by an actress— Ingrid Bergman in the role of Gladys Aylward, an English missionary to China. I doubt that many women will see this picture through with dry cheeks, though it is not a tragedy but puts its stress on human warmth.

Bosley Crowther in The New York Times:

Ingrid Bergman's capacity to convey a sense of supreme sincerity with little more to work with in the way of a character than a simple and wholesome facade is touchingly demonstrated.

John McCarten in The New Yorker:

Perhaps Miss Bergman, all aglow with health and beauty, doesn't look like the sort of lady who might decide to devote her energies to missionary work, but as the film goes along, she

radiates such honesty that we are willing to believe anything she wants us to.

In Saturday Review:

Miss Bergman's performance is expert. . . . There are times when the story moves slowly, but more bothersome, perhaps, is its predictability. One is sure that Miss Bergman will always rise to the occasion, whatever the challenge. There is therefore no surprise, not even suspense, when she does.

With Anthony Perkins

Goodbye Again

(Aimez-Vous Brahms?)

United Artists, 1961

CAST

Ingrid Bergman, Yves Montand, Anthony Perkins, Jessie Royce Landis, Jackie Lane, Pierre Dux, Jean Clarke, Peter Bull, Michele Mercier, Uta Taeger, Andre Randall, David Horne, Lee Patrick, A. Duperoux, Raymond Gerome, Jean Hebey, Michel Garland, Paul Uny, Colin Mann, Diahann Carroll.

CREDITS

An Anatole Litvak production released through United Artists. Directed by Anatole Litvak. Screenplay by Samuel Taylor, based on the novel Aimez-Vous Brahms? by Françoise Sagan. Music by Georges Auric. Lyrics by Dory Langdon. Photographed by Armand Thirard. Miss Bergman's gowns by Christian Dior. Produced at Studios de Boulogne, France. Running time, 120 minutes.

THE STORY

Paula Tessier (Ingrid Bergman) is an aging Parisian interior decorator who is involved with an also-aging but stll man-about-townish Roger Demarest (Yves Montand). Roger dates Paula regularly, but of late has tended to leave her at her door without coming in, while he saves his more intimate favors for comely younger women. Insecure and lonely, and fearful that she is losing her hold on Roger and that he will never marry her, forty-year-old Paula finds herself unwilling to resist the persistent courting of young Philip Van Der Besh (Anthony Perkins) who is fifteen years her junior. Rich American socialite Mrs. Van Der Besh (Jessie Royce Landis), Philip's mother, suspects her son's infatuation with Paula, who finds the situation embarrassing because Mrs. Van Der Besh is one of her important clients.

With Yves Montand

At first Paula tries sincerely to discourage Philip, as she still loves Roger, despite his neglect and his unaccountable cancellations of dinner engagements because of "pressing business." Philip learns that Roger is two-timing Paula constantly, and this encourages him to pursue her more aggressively. Roger and his current date encounter Philip and Paula at a nightclub and this temporarily resparks Roger's interest in Paula. But Paula, as usual wearing her heart on her sleeve, returns to him without resistance, and Roger soon loses interest again. Philip, now sincerely in love with Paula, courts her openly at a party and Roger leaves in anger. When Roger refuses to let Paula accompany him on his next trip, she finally turns to Philip—especially after she finds he has waited, cold and wet and dazed, for hours outside her shop. When Roger returns he finds that Paula and Philip are having a full-fledged affair and that Philip has moved in with her.

Instead of trying to win her back with tenderness, Roger turns from her in anger and outraged pride. He tries to forget Paula with different women but it doesn't work. Nor is Philip really the answer for Paula, who realizes she has taken up with the boy out of her loneliness and need to be loved. When Roger finally comes to her and tells her he cannot live without her, she returns to him. She tries to tell Philip as tactfully and kindly as possible, but the boy, heartbroken and bewildered, rushes from the apartment and out of her life. Roger decides to do "the right thing" by Paula, and they are married. But the night soon comes when Roger phones her that he is "detained on business" and Paula, realizing that she has lost both men and that she is now truly alone, gazes at her stricken face in the dressing-room mirror.

REVIEWS

Lawrence J. Quirk in Screen Slants:

The idea of a middle-aged woman finding happiness, however temporary, with a young man is not the sort of thing that certain emotionally-immature elements of the American audience find appealing—yet it happens in real life with a fair amount of regularity. Ingrid Bergman, her radiant womanliness never more evident, and her acting sincere and feelingful, helps Anthony Perkins to make more than his usual contribution. What Greta Garbo did for an erstwhile-

163

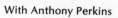
With Anthony Perkins

With Jessie Royce-Landis and
Yves Montand

With Anthony Perkins

callow Robert Taylor in *Camille* and Bette Davis did for a hitherto-wooden Glenn Ford in *A Stolen Life*, Miss Bergman does for Mr. Perkins here. He has caught a spark from her magical artistry and her mature creative insights, and shows himself more warm, expressive and human than I have seen him do since his sensitive performance in 1954 as John Kerr's replacement in *Tea and Sympathy* on Broadway. Of course this is one of those pictures that are foreordained for an unhappy ending, life and love being the perverse, unpredictable things they are, and a fadeout of Miss Bergman staring into a dressing-table mirror at her aging aloneness is one of those movie moments that will linger in any sensitive, responsive viewer's memory.

Dilys Powell in The Sunday Times (London):

The indestructible inner grace of *(Miss Berg-* *man)* wins me every time, and here she is at her most magical.

In Saturday Review:

The loves, the hopes, the despairs of the woman of forty are elegantly . . . set forth. Miss Bergman handles the forty-year-old Paula with some accomplished artifice.

Vincent Canby in Variety:

The beauty of Miss Bergman's performance illuminates, and adds validity to, the . . . fiction.

Bosley Crowther in The New York Times:

Miss Bergman does ooze great anxiety, compassion and dignity, and she gives a nice impression of being devoted to the Frenchman, Yves Montand.

Ingrid Bergman

The Visit

20th Century-Fox, 1964

CAST

Ingrid Bergman, Anthony Quinn, Irina Demick, Valentina Cortese, Ernest Schroeder, Paolo Stoppa, Hans-Christian Bleck, Romolo Valli, Claude Dauphin, Eduardo Ciannelli, Leonard Stoeckel, Richard Munch, Mario Guglielmi, Jacques Dufilho, Fausto Tozzi, Dante Meggio, Reno Palmer, Lelia Luttozzi.

CREDITS

Produced by Julian Derode. Directed by Bernhard Wicki. From the screenplay by Ben Barzman based on the play by Friedrich Duerrenmatt. Photographed by Armando Nannuzzi and Claudio Cirillo. Music by Hans-Martin Majewski. Art director: Leon Barsacq. Miss Bergman's costumes designed by Rene Hubert and executed by Nini Ricci. Set decorator: Robert Christides. Film editor: Sam Beetley. Produced in black and white CinemaScope, at Cinecitta Studios, Rome. Running time, 100 minutes.

THE STORY

Karla Zachanassian (Ingrid Bergman), the richest woman in the world, returns to her home town of Guellen, in Central Europe, twenty years after she has left it, to wreak a unique form of long-delayed vengeance. She seeks the ruination of Serge Miller (Anthony Quinn), the town's leading merchant, who two decades before had

166

With Anthony Quinn

seduced and then betrayed her, denying the paternity of her unborn child, and allowing her to be run out of town.

Friendless and homeless, Karla had turned to prostitution after the death of her child. Later her fortunes had risen, and she had married a multi-millionaire whose death left her financially all-powerful. Now, on her visit home, she sets out to turn the townspeople against Miller by offering them a million marks for the town, another million to be divided among the people, if they will give her "justice"—the life of Serge Miller.

The townsfolk are at first repelled by the idea, then gradually their cupidity takes over, as they persuade themselves that their poverty, and the promised alleviation of it by Karla, warrant their putting the increasingly frightened Serge on trial and condemning him to death. Karla, who still retains a vestige of love for Serge, encounters a servant girl, Anya *(Irina Demick)*, who is in love with a married gendarme. Seeing herself in the girl, as she was twenty years before, Karla encourages her to leave the town and provides her with the means to do it. Serge's wife, Mathilda *(Valentina Cortese)*, proves loyal to him only up to a point, and the townspeople of Guellen, now driven to a pitch of rationalizing, malevolent greed, win Karla's ultimate contempt by almost killing Serge.

But Karla steps in at the last minute, and spares her erstwhile lover's life. She has decided that she does not wish to make a martyr of him, and prefers to let him live out his life racked by guilt, shame, and the knowledge of his fellow-townsmen's betrayal of him. (In the play, Karla left Serge to his fate.)

REVIEWS

Lee Beaupre in the New York Express:

Miss Bergman's performance is in every respect splendid: her bearing is stylishly theatrical, her inflections emotionally muted, her mannerisms both superficially charming and essentially sinister.

In Newsweek:

Miss Bergman is convincingly scornful and vindictive. . . . Bernhard Wicki's direction is crisp and straightforward. . . . Duerrenmatt has taken the old idea of a woman scorned and has used it to express what depths of spite and malignancy are hidden in us all.

Kate Cameron in the New York Daily News:

In writing of the play, John Chapman said it was cut to fit the personalities of the stars *(Lunt* and *Fontanne)* but in revamping it to the screen,

With Anthony Quinn

With Irina Demick (right)

it was not recut for the talents of either Ingrid Bergman or Anthony Quinn.

Judith Crist in the New York Herald Tribune:

. . . Friedrich Duerrenmatt's stunning chiller, made more so by the Lunts on Broadway in 1958, has come to the screen and been turned into a run-of-the-mill morality melodrama. Larger than life on stage though the screen may be, particularly in CinemaScope, the film has reduced this grisly horror story of greed and betrayal to the trivial, plotted terms of a woman's vengeance. The slow, civilized, deceptively gentle weaving of a surrealist fantasy of evil has become a matter of plot mechanics. The play's macabre quality has evaporated and the attempted realism of Bernhard Wicki's directorial approach seems only to underline its absence.

A. H. Weiler in The New York Times:

Friedrich Duerrenmatt's *The Visit,* which swept Broadway like a searching wind six years ago, has changed direction and lost a good deal of force in its journey to the screen. The Swiss playwright's cutting cynicism and Machiavellian logic have not lost their sharpness in this dissection of justice and man's inhumanity to man. But in softening a grim, yet rational, denouement and in a largely pedestrian approach to shattering drama, *The Visit* has veered from harsh but memorable reality to careful theatricality that does not become a matter of life and death. . . . As the woman of everlasting hate who still loves the man who disgraced and rejected her, Ingrid Bergman is as comely, stately and regal as becomes one of Europe's wealthiest women. However, the logic of her plan notwithstanding, she is more often a strident woman, emotionally rather than intellectually involved with someone who does not seem worth all this trouble.

The Yellow Rolls-Royce

Metro-Goldwyn-Mayer, 1965

CAST

Ingrid Bergman, Omar Sharif, Joyce Grenfell, Wally Cox.

CREDITS

Produced by Anatole de Grunwald. Directed by Anthony Asquith. Screenplay by Terence Rattigan. Photographed by Jack Hildyard. Musical score by Riz Ortolani. Editor: Frank Clarke. Produced in Panavision and MetroColor. (Third of three episodes, each running about forty minutes, of a film with a total running time of 122 minutes.)

NOTE

This three-part episode film concerned three successive owners of a Rolls-Royce, which figures in all three plots. Episode I featured Rex Harrison, Jeanne Moreau, Edmund Purdom,

Moira Lister, Isa Miranda and Roland Culver. Episode II featured Shirley MacLaine, Alain Delon, George C. Scott and Art Carney.

THE STORY

Three episodes are tied together by successive ownership of a Rolls-Royce, which figures prominently in all the stories. In Episode I, the Marquess of Frinton (*Rex Harrison*) buys the yellow and black town car for his beautiful wife, the Marchioness (*Jeanne Moreau*) and presents it to her during a dinner party they are giving at their country estate. The Marchioness is carrying on a secret affair with her husband's aide, John Fane (*Edmund Purdom*). The Marchioness' secret is discovered by Lady St. Simeon (*Moira Lister*), who cues in the Marquess on the goings-on between his wife and Fane while they are all at the Ascot Races. The Marquess finds his wife and Fane embracing in the town car, is deeply hurt, and though he continues the marriage, he immediately disposes of the car. In Episode II, Mafia bigwig Paolo Maltese (*George C. Scott*) and his girlfriend, Mac Jenkins (*Shirley MacLaine*), are touring Italy with Maltese's henchman Joey (*Art Carney*). The trio encounter Stefano, a photographer (*Alain Delon*), who makes up to Mac and

With Omar Sharif

is sent away by Maltese. Later Maltese goes to America to liquidate a Mafia recalcitrant, leaving Mac in the care of Joey. Mac again encounters Stefano and a romance develops which is tol-

With Omar Sharif

170

With Omar Sharif

With Omar Sharif

With Omar Sharif

erated by the understanding Joey. Later Maltese returns and Joey makes Mac realize that the only way she can save Stefano from Maltese's jealous vengeance is to pretend to Stefano that she no longer loves him, and go back to Maltese, which she does. In Episode III, Mrs. Gerda Millett *(Ingrid Bergman),* a wealthy American widow, is preparing to leave Trieste in early 1941 en route to Belgrade to visit the Queen Mother. She meets up with Darich, a Yugoslav *(Omar Sharif),* who persuades her that he is an anti-Communist organizer and gets her help in reentering Yugoslavia. Actually he is a Yugoslav partisan who wants to help fight the Germans in the impending Nazi invasion, which breaks out as he and Gerda are in a hotel dining room in a small Yugoslavian town. Gerda helps rescue the wounded, uses her town car for transporting partisan guerrillas and aids them in their movements, driving the car herself. In the process she wins Darich's respect, and eventually his love. After a night of lovemaking in the town car, they go on to a village, which they help liberate. Then Darich tells her they must part, as her country is not yet involved in the war against the Germans. He asks Gerda to tell her fellow-Americans what is taking place in Yugoslavia. Gerda goes back to Italy, but she knows she will never forget Darich and their experiences together.

REVIEWS

A. H. Weiler in The New York Times:

In the 60 years of its existence, Britain's Rolls-Royce justifiably has become the Kohinoor of cars, the utmost in custom-built elegance, efficiency and price, the conveyance of kings and the envy of mechanics. But *The Yellow Rolls-Royce* which arrived yesterday at the Music Hall fresh from Metro-Goldwyn-Mayer's European works, performs, despite its color, opulence and surface polish, largely like an assembly-line job. It is, it should be stressed, a pretty slick vehicle; that is, pleasing to the eye and occasionally amusing, but it hardly seems worthy of all the effort and the noted personalities involved in the glossy but superficial stories that make up this shiny package. One is reminded of the new classic Rolls-Royce advertising slogan, "The loudest noise comes from the clock." In this *Yellow Rolls-Royce* there is very little that jolts, shocks, excites or surprises. Terence Rattigan's original screenplay is devoted to three separate yarns tied together only by the separate owners of the same beautiful, titular town car. . . . Miss Bergman and Omar

With Omar Sharif

Sharif manage to give this somewhat improbable [third episode] a lift by energetic and humorous delineations. . . . Miss Bergman's unrestrained dowager is forceful and impressive, despite a somewhat contrived situation.

In Screen Stars:

The locations span England, Italy and Yugoslavia, and it is obvious that no expense was spared in any of the shooting. The audience, however, sits on the edge of its seats, waiting for titillations which for some reason are all too few, but not knowing exactly whom or what to blame. Verdict: Lavish production, so-so drama.

Kenneth Tynan in The London Observer:

My immediate reaction to Ingrid Bergman's performance as the spunky "chauffeuse" was to suspect that the part had been written for Katharine Hepburn, and to be absolutely sure that if such was the case, Miss Hepburn had been right to turn it down.

In Saturday Review:

Terence Rattigan put together this surefire blend of sentiment, humor and mock heroics, and he has done it deftly if superficially.

In the London Sunday Telegraph:

[The Yellow Rolls-Royce] looks less like a film than an investment, laden with everything that money can buy. Anyone willing to be taken for a smooth ride could hardly find a more sumptuous vehicle, star-studded, gold-plated, shockproof and probably critic-proof, too.

Stimulantia

Omnia Film, 1967

(An eight-part film featuring episodes directed by Hans Abramson, Jorn Donner, Lars Gorling, Ingmar Bergman, Arne Arnbom, Tage Danielsson-Hans Alfredson, Gustaf Molander, who directed some of Miss Bergman's first Swedish films, and Vilgot Sjoman. Miss Bergman appeared in the episode directed by Molander.)

Smycket

(The Necklace)

CAST

Ingrid Bergman, Gunnar Bjornstrand, Gunnel Brostrom.

CREDITS

Written and directed by Gustaf Molander from the tale by Guy de Maupassant. Photography: Gunnar Fischer, F.S.F.

NOTE

"Smycket" was made by Miss Bergman in Sweden in the fall of 1964. Molander was then seventy-seven. It was photographed in the same studio of the Swedish Film Industry where her first film was made. She had the same dressing room and some of the original crew were on hand.

THE STORY

The wife *(Ingrid Bergman)* of a government clerk *(Gunnar Bjornstrand)* longs for a more expensive and luxurious life-style. A woman of taste and refined habits, she was born below the station her talents and appearance warranted,

With Gunnel Brostrom

and she has married a man of limited potential who is incapable of helping her to fulfill her dreams. She wistfully envies her rich friend (Gunnel Brostrom), who has beautiful clothes and fine jewels, and sees as little as possible of her because she feels inferior and deprived. Her husband wangles an invitation to a government reception and ball, but the wife doesn't wish to attend because she hasn't the right clothes and doesn't want to look poor beside the other women. Her husband sacrifices money he had put aside for a hunting trip to buy her a presentable gown. But she feels that she will not be able to compete with the other ladies unless she is also wearing a tasteful ornament. Her husband suggests that she ask her friend to lend her a piece of jewelry. She is given her choice of jewels by her friend and chooses a beautiful diamond necklace. She wears it to the ball and is the hit of the evening, sought after by the men and admired by all.

But when she and her husband arrive home after what has probably been the happiest evening of her life, she finds that she has lost the necklace. Her husband retraces their journey but the necklace is irretrievably lost. Terrified, the pair search through various jewelry shops until they find one they think is quite similar and equally expensive, and then the wife returns it to her friend, passing it off as the original. For the next ten years, the couple scrimp and save and pay heavy, usurious notes to defray the cost of the expensive necklace. Their life has become abject and bitterly hard as a result.

One day the wife, now drab and old beyond her years, meets the friend who lent her the necklace. She decides to tell her of the ten years of deprivation she and her husband went through to make good on the necklace. To her horror, her friend tells her that it was only a worthless paste imitation.

REVIEWS

In Aftenposten (Norwegian):

Marvelous acting by Ingrid Bergman and Gunnar Bjornstrand turns ["Smycket"] into an intermezzo one will long remember.

In Chaplin (Swedish):

According to his own statement, this is Gustaf Molander's final film. It is a sober account in the best Svensk-Filmindustri tradition. . . . No surprises here, that's for sure. But Ingrid Bergman is beautiful.

In Expressen (Swedish):

Gustaf Molander has Maupassant and Ingrid Bergman, and, with the right that age commands,

With Gunnar Bjornstrand

the largest slice of the cake. Accordingly, this slice appears to be baked in a different world. Ingrid Bergman is beautiful and the crystals ring when she speaks.

In Aftonbladet (Swedish):

Should one use words such as beautiful and competent, it is not only to Ingrid Bergman that the reference is made in her role as the . . . civil servant's wife whose hunger for life has long outgrown her husband's salary. No, it is mainly a question here of Molander's firm hand as regards period style and his talent for the pastiche, his way of forging . . . the story and finally resolving it in a denouement which he develops fulfillingly. Ah, for the balance and for the true and firm eye that is shown by this veteran. . . .

With Gunnar Bjornstrand

176

Cactus Flower

Columbia, 1969

CAST

Ingrid Bergman, Walter Matthau, Goldie Hawn, Jack Weston, Rick Lenz, Vito Scotti, Irene Hervey, Eve Bruce, Irwin Charone, Matthew Saks.

CREDITS

Produced by M. J. Frankovich. Directed by Gene Saks. Screenplay by I. A. L. Diamond from the stage play by Abe Burrows, based on a French play by Barillet and Gredy. Director of photography: Charles E. Lang, A.S.C. Music by *Quincy Jones. Film editor: Maury Winetrobe. Color by Technicolor. Running time, 103 minutes.*

THE STORY

Stephanie Dickinson *(Ingrid Bergman)* is the unnoticed and essentially unappreciated assistant to bachelor dentist Julian Winston *(Walter Matthau),* who fancies himself in love with a much-younger Greenwich Village kook, Toni Simmons *(Goldie Hawn),* who is in turn pursued by a

With Goldie Hawn, Walter Matthau and Jack Weston

young writer next door, Igor Sullivan *(Rick Lenz)*. When Julian asks Stephanie to pose as his wife to dupe Toni into thinking he is a married man with several children, Stephanie decides to refurbish her drab and forbidding exterior and doll herself up to attract Julian, with whom she has been secretly in love for some years. Julian asks her to continue posing as his wife and persuades her to appear in public with his friend, Harvey Greenfield *(Jack Weston)*, and Toni, so as to convince a suddenly contrite and guilt-ridden Toni that his "wife" wants a divorce and is also playing around.

Toni, Julian, Stephanie and Harvey meet at a nightclub where Stephanie exhibits a newfound sparkle, to the annoyance of Julian who is reluctantly developing a long-deferred interest in her. Stephanie does a wild bugaloo with Igor, and then with Toni. Eventually Stephanie tells an increasingly confused Toni that she is not Julian's wife but only his office assistant, and when Toni traps Julian into a continuing lie, she turns at last to the patiently waiting Igor. Julian realizes that Stephanie is really his true love and they embrace.

REVIEWS

Rela. in Variety:

The film . . . drags, which is probably the worst thing that can be said of a light comedy. . . . The plot is minimal and the lines are somewhat stilted and hollow, but if the direction was tighter and the mood kept light and airy, it might have worked. . . . Production values are all good, except that the film is so slow in spots that one wonders why Quincy Jones didn't add more music. . . . All in all, it is good to see Miss Bergman back on the screen. Her scenes as the nurse are okay but she blossoms, as does the character, when out of uniform and on a discotheque dance floor. She's still a very desirable woman. . . . It's always unfair to compare a film to its stage version, especially since many millions will see the film who are unfamiliar with the play. The film should stand alone. In that respect, *Cactus Flower* is mildly amusing.

Lawrence J. Quirk in Screen Slants:

Miss Bergman has been extremely well photo-

graphed by cameraman Charles E. Lang and looks remarkably youthful and fresh in Technicolor. She exhibits a sharp comedy sense throughout the proceedings, and when she competes with cute little Goldie Hawn on a discotheque dance floor, both of them executing their individual ideas of what constitutes a wild bugaloo—well, things percolate! She is drab and dreary and unloved as the ugly-duckling dental assistant; glamorous and sparkling and chicly gowned as the swan-like, sought-after nightspot habitue. All in all, a tour-de-force for the indefatigable Bergman, and it is good to have this two-time Oscar winner back on the American screen.

Wanda Hale in the New York Daily News:

Cactus Flower has the comedy mark of Gene Saks on it, all right, but not the steady flow of artful humor skillfully injected by this director into *The Odd Couple* and *Barefoot in the Park*. This doesn't mean that *Cactus Flower* is not a

With Walter Matthau

funny picture. There are laughs enough. . . . Miss Bergman lets her inhibitions down and becomes the swingiest swinger of a swinging set. Heretofore unnoticed, she becomes the desirable woman, adored by all men, including her boss. And audiences will love her for getting in there and providing more laughs than anybody. Goldie Hawn is so funny for awhile, you think she will steal the show, but you change your mind when Bergman puts her mind to the comedy in her role.

Howard Thompson in The New York Times:

It is primarily the verve and skill of the performances, the pungent air of sexual chemistry and the peppery good humor that make the movie so diverting. Neither the wisecracks, old and new and generally funny, nor the characterizations seem as bland as on Broadway. The teaming of Matthau, whose dour, craggy virility now supplants the easy charm of Barry Nelson, and the ultra-feminine Miss Bergman, in a rare comedy venture, was inspirational on somebody's part. The lady is delightful as a (now) "Swedish iceberg," no longer young, who flowers radiantly while running interference for the boss's romantic bumbling. The two stars mesh perfectly.

Archer Winsten in the New York Post:

The surprise of the casting, of course, is Ingrid Bergman, and she's a pleasant one. As an efficient secretary, she's right on target, and when circumstances call for her to display the tribal-rock side of her personality, she gives it a good college try. That's all right. If she did more, it would be too much.

180

With Anthony Quinn

A Walk in the Spring Rain

Columbia, 1970

CAST

Ingrid Bergman, Anthony Quinn, Fritz Weaver, Katherine Crawford, Tom Fielding, Virginia Gregg, Mitchell Silberman.

CREDITS

A Stirling Silliphant-Guy Green Production. Directed by Guy Green. Written for the screen and produced by Stirling Silliphant. Based on the novel by Rachel Maddux. Director of photography: Charles B. Lang, A.S.C. Filmed in Panavision. Color by Technicolor. Film editor: Ferris Webster. Art director: Malcolm C. Bert. Miss Bergman's wardrobe by Donfeld. Music by Elmer Bernstein. Title song by Elmer Bernstein and Don Black. Title song sung by Michael Dees. Running time, 98 minutes.

THE STORY

Roger Meredith *(Fritz Weaver)*, a university professor, and his wife, Libby *(Ingrid Bergman)*, leave their home in New York City for the hills of eastern Tennessee, where Roger plans to write a book on sabbatical from his academic duties. Roger and Libby have a daughter, Ellen *(Katherine Crawford)*, who is studying law, and a grandson, Bucky *(Mitchell Silberman)*.

Libby is intelligent, sensitive and aware, and she finds the uncomplicated atmosphere and ways of the people of eastern Tennessee a refreshing change from the harried big-city life she has known. The Merediths meet Will Cade *(Anthony Quinn)*, a neighbor and handyman, married like herself but with an earthy heartiness and virile magnetism that her scholarly, detached husband lacks. Will and Libby are attracted to each other, the attraction deepens into love, and soon Libby is ridden with guilt and an ominous sense that no happiness can come of it.

She tries to reestablish a rapport with her husband while on a trip to a nearby town, but Roger is a phlegmatic, self-centered type wrapped up in his book, and Libby craves the wholehearted, unselfish love that Will offers. Will's son Boy *(Tom Fielding)* a combative, restless young man, sees Will and Libby from a distance during one of their more tender interludes and becomes cynical and hostile toward them both. Ellen suddenly joins her parents in eastern Tennessee and asks Libby to return to New York to care for Bucky while Ellen attends Harvard Law School. Libby, reluctant to leave Will and her newfound happiness, tells her daughter that she, too, despite the encroachments of middle age, wants to live and be happy. But Libby is troubled.

Boy approaches Libby on a lonely country road and cynically attempts to make love to her. Will comes along, sees them, and kills his son accidentally in a fight while the horrified Libby looks on.

Shattered by Boy's death, Will turns all the more to Libby, but at this point Roger, who senses their estrangement, asks Libby to return

With Tom Fielding

With Anthony Quinn and Tom Fielding

with him to New York. Libby, realizing that there is no future for her and Will, and that their love has come too late in life, goes back to New York with Roger and assumes the care of her grandson while Ellen is at Harvard. Will has told her that he will always be there waiting for her, should she change her mind. But Libby knows in her heart that her last chance at love has gone and that she must settle for whatever compensations middle age offers.

REVIEWS
Lawrence J. Quirk in Screen Slants:

As the middle-aged, affection-starved wife of a university professor who finds herself trapped in a prosaic, dull and unromantic marriage, Ingrid Bergman gives an affecting, poignant and sincere performance, and she has wisely elected to underplay her more dramatic and emotional scenes. Transplanted from New York to eastern Tennessee when her husband, played with effectively-obtuse pomposity by Fritz Weaver, decides to write a book there on sabbatical from his teaching duties, she proves to be a lonely, heart-hungry push-over for the love proffered by virile backwoodsman Anthony Quinn, who provides the warm emotion and thorough commitment that her husband denies her. Miss Bergman out-acts the usually-vital Quinn, who seems uncharacteristically subdued here.

She is, in fact, better by far than the film itself, for it has been rather indifferently written and produced by Stirling Silliphant and directed by

Guy Green with a lack of sharpness and a slackness of approach that fails to take full advantage of the more climactic moments. Indeed, whatever sharpness and romantic power the film possesses can be credited to Miss Bergman, who seems to be dragging the film along with the force of a sleek diesel hitched to a set of toy trolley cars.

Even so, this is not among her top performances; even a consummate artist must be sustained by proper direction and a polished script, and she has neither here. Best of her fellow performers is newcomer Tom Fielding as Quinn's embittered son. In fact, Miss Bergman's skillfully intense underplaying and Fielding's toughly-impassioned eloquence are the only two plusses this rather pedestrian drama can honestly boast. A shame, too, for the theme—that the middle-aged have as much right to romantic love as the young—is a valid one. Mr. Silliphant will have to content himself with an A for good intentions and a C for execution.

Howard Thompson in The New York Times:

A dreary, tedious, unconvincing drama of middle-aged love . . . [it] should have been a beauty. It's a bore. And the saddest thing about it is Miss Bergman's hope, as expressed in the film's promotion, for another *Brief Encounter*. The picture moves self-consciously, like mountain molasses. . . . [It] is a sketchily overstated exercise of no urgency and precious little warmth. . . . Striving mightily and looking lovely, Miss Bergman seems merely a petulant woman who falls into the arms of Quinn for novelty, from boredom. . . .

Archer Winsten in the New York Post:

Anthony Quinn and Ingrid Bergman are left out there wrestling with a script they can't quite make human and habitable.

Frank Leyendecker in Greater Amusements:

Ingrid Bergman reverts to the type of portrayal which made her famous, a warm, human and sympathetic dramatic role which she plays superbly, as always. . . . This is primarily a "woman's picture," with its strongest appeal to mature moviegoers who will better appreciate the romance between the matronly Miss Bergman and Anthony Quinn.

Richard Cohen in Women's Wear Daily:

Ingrid Bergman [gives] a serviceable but wasted performance. . . . The romance is cluttered up by side forays into the generation conflict, one of the contemporary themes now seen as necessary to an up-to-date movie. *(Katherine Crawford)* assures her mother *(Miss Bergman)*, seething with passion for her mountain lover *(Mr. Quinn)*, that at her age she (the mother) has found "peace of mind." The mother opts for baby-sitterdom. It made me ashamed for middle-aged folks.

Wanda Hale in the New York Daily News:

Ingrid Bergman . . . looks so lovely and gives a touching impersonation of a married woman who has a brief interlude with a man the direct opposite of her scholarly husband. . . . Men will fall in love with Miss Bergman. Everybody can fall in love with the scenic grandeur but we all cannot fall completely in love with the bitter-sweet story of middle-aged love.

Stage Appearances

Liliom

1940

CAST

Burgess Meredith, Ingrid Bergman, Margaret Wycherly, John Emery, Ann Mason, Elia Kazan, Frank Vincent, Joseph Kramm, Beatrice Pearson, Elaine Perry, Evelyn Moser, Jane Amor, Joseph McCauley, Howard Freeman, Frank Vincent, Kenneth Bates, Francis de Sales, Lee Bergman, Chet Rue, Gibbs Penrose, Arnold Karff, Joan Tetzel, Richard Mackay.

CREDITS

A play in a prologue and two acts by Ferenc Molnar. Adapted by Benjamin Glazer. Staged by Benno Schneider. Settings, costumes and lighting by Nat Karson. Incidental music by Deems Taylor. Presented at the Forty-Fourth Street Theatre on March 25, 1940 by Vinton Freedley.

THE STORY

Liliom *(Burgess Meredith)* is a Budapest carnival tough, a vulgar and insensitive lout who follows the path of least resistance. After losing his post, he marries a servant girl, Julie *(Ingrid Bergman)*, who is going to have his child. Julie deeply loves Liliom, and idealizes him, though he treats her unkindly, beats her, and provides for her inadequately. He dies in an attempted robbery, having committed suicide to escape inevitable arrest, and the heavenly authorities try to combat his proud and stubborn and unrepentant nature by sending him back to earth sixteen years later, where he is told to try to do one good deed. Liliom finds Julie and his now-grown daughter still poverty-stricken and struggling, and is irritated to learn that his wife has brought up his daughter to idealize him. Disguised as a mendicant, Liliom tells the girl the truth about himself, and in desperation slaps her. The heavenly authorities are annoyed, but the girl gets the intimation that the slap was more like a kiss than a blow. For it was the only way that the loutish Liliom could register either concern or affection.

REVIEWS

Richard Watts, Jr., in the
New York Herald Tribune:

Miss Bergman brings a fresh, clean quality to the theatre that is entirely charming, and she

plays with grace and forthright honesty. . . . I hope Miss Bergman does not rush back to Hollywood too soon.

Burns Mantle in the New York Daily News:

Last night it seemed to me that Ingrid Bergman, pretty Swedish motion picture actress, making her American stage debut in the role, was the warmest and most satisfying of the Julies [I have seen] and the least peasant-like in the part. . . . It is nice to have Miss Bergman about. She is honest, sensitive and carefully schooled.

Brooks Atkinson in The New York Times:

The part of Julie introduces us to a young actress of extraordinary gifts and ability. Ingrid Bergman comes from Stockholm. Although she recently appeared in the screenplay *Intermezzo*, this is her first appearance on the English-speaking stage. She has a slight accent. She also has a clean-cut beauty of figure and manner, responsive eyes, a sensitive mouth, a pleasant voice that can be heard and modulated. And more than that, she seems to have complete command of the part she is playing. Although Julie is shy and somewhat taciturn, Miss Bergman keeps the part wholly alive and lightens it from within with luminous beauty.

Sidney B. Whipple in the New York World-Telegram:

There is a certain peasant freshness about Miss

Bergman's performance that instantly captures your sympathy, and there is a dignity and power in the more emotional scenes that wins your profound respect as well.

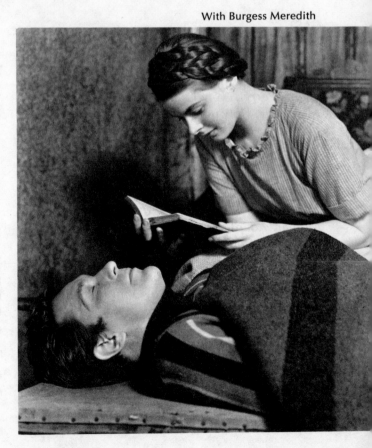

With David O. Selznick, whose Selznick Company produced *Anna Christie*

Anna Christie

1941

CAST

Ingrid Bergman, Damian O'Flynn, Jessie Bosley, J. Edward Bromberg, John Miller, Peter Bronte, Edmund Glover, Walter Brooke, William Alland.

CREDITS

A play by Eugene O'Neill. Produced by The Selznick Company under the direction of John Houseman and Alfred de Liagre, Jr. Directed by John Houseman. Production designed by Kate Drain Lawson from sketches by William Cameron Menzies. Opened at the Lobero Theatre, Santa Barbara, California, and played July 30-31 and August 1-2. Opened at the Curran Theatre, San Francisco, California, August 4, 1941. In September the play was seen at the Maplewood Theatre, Maplewood, N. J. Directed by Margaret Webster,

it featured Art Smith as Chris Christopherson and Clare Woodbury as Marthy Owen. Damian O'Flynn repeated his role at Mat Burke.

THE STORY

Anna Christie *(Ingrid Bergman)* returns after fifteen years to visit her father, Chris Christopherson *(J. Edward Bromberg)*, captain of a coal barge. Seduced at sixteen by a cousin, and besieged by ill health, Anna had drifted into a life of prostitution. Now she wants to get one last chance from life. After meeting an old female salt, Marthy Owen *(Jessie Bosley)* a friend of her father's, in a waterfront saloon, Anna and her father are reunited, though she reproaches him bitterly for his neglect over the years. Anna goes to live with her father on his barge, and they

learn to know each other all over again. Once on the open water, the barge picks up a shipwrecked sailor, Mat Burke *(Damian O'Flynn)*, a stoker, who falls in love with Anna and wants to marry her. Determined to be honest, Anna tells both her father and her suitor of her former life, and when Mat rejects her bitterly, she despairs. But Mat, after going on a drinking spree with Chris, who has likewise been shocked by Anna's revelations, comes back and tells Anna that he still loves her. Anna promises to wait for her father and her suitor, who have signed up for a ship voyage.

REVIEW

M. S. in The New York Times:

The production marks the fulfillment of a long-time dream of Mr. Selznick to provide Southern California with its own summer theatre—"strawhat" is a shade too bucolic for the affair in hand—and it can be reported with considerable relief and pleasure that the current production offers the hope that at last a professional, adult theatre, so often promised but never really achieved, might be coming out of Hollywood. A gentleman of undisputed taste in the matter of motion pictures, Mr. Selznick has brought that same quality to his theatrical endeavor, and has surrounded himself with people who not only know their way around the theatre but know how to treat it with respect. . . . To this spectator it seemed that Miss Bergman, an excellent actress and a lovely young woman, made an interesting, and at many times a touching, Anna, but that she was prevented by qualities instinct in her person from realizing the depths of utter degradation and defeat of O'Neill's wretched girl. Her own windswept cleanliness of body and spirit seemed to shine through, despite a really good performance ably directed.

Joan of Lorraine

1946

CAST

Ingrid Bergman, Sam Wanamaker, Kenneth Tobey, Gilmore Brush, Lewis Martin, Bruce Hall, Charles Ellis, Arthur L. Sachs, Peter Hobbs, Barry Kroeger, Romney Brent, Lynn Kearse, Roger De Koven, Harry Irvine, Kevin McCarthy, Martin Rudy, Brooks West, Ann Coray, Joanna Roos, Joseph Wiseman, Stephen Roberts, Lotte Stavisky.

CREDITS

A play by Maxwell Anderson in two acts. Presented by The Playwright's Company. Directed by Margo Jones. Settings, lighting and costumes by Lee Simonson. Presented at the Alvin Theatre on November 18, 1946.

NOTE

For her performance in this play Miss Bergman received the Antoinette Perry Award.

THE STORY

Actress Mary Grey (Ingrid Bergman) has been assigned the title role in a production of Joan of Arc. She arrives for rehearsals on an almost-bare stage, where the action of the play takes place, primarily as a series of rehearsals, interspersed with scenes depicting the rise, triumph and fall of The Maid. These are acted against sparse backgrounds without costuming.

With Kevin McCarthy, Harry Irvine, Roger De Koven, Martin Rudy, and Romney Brent (seated)

In the play depicted during the rehearsal, Joan of Arc compromises with the politicians who seek to discredit her and disprove her mission. This seems unnatural, indeed unacceptable, to Mary Grey, who pauses during her interpretation to take issue with the director *(Sam Wanamaker)* as to the motivations and characterization of Joan and her persecutors.

Rehearsals come to a stop as Mary, the director and others discuss the mystique of the play, often in argumentative and heated terms. Determined to interpret the role as she sees fit, Mary Grey walks off the stage at one point, and her differences with the director seem bitter and irremediable. However, she returns, and in the middle of one scene, she comes to realize the truth: that compromises have been made by her heroine Joan on non-essential matters while all the time she holds fast to what is unchangeable and non-negotiable.

She realizes now that compromises on unimportant points can and must sometimes be made if the living are to maintain what ideals they have. Compromise, in other words, can have its place in the practical, but not in the spiritual, world. (Wanamaker doubled in the role of the director of the rehearsal and the Inquisitor

in the play itself. Many moving and climactic scenes from the life of Joan of Arc are depicted in scenes interspersed with the rehearsal activities and arguments set forth.)

REVIEWS

Brooks Atkinson in The New York Times:

. . . There is no doubt about the splendor of Miss Bergman's acting. It fills the theatre with unaccustomed radiance. Six years ago Miss Bergman paused briefly in New York to play in a revival of *Liliom* en route to Hollywood. Her beauty was extraordinary then, and her gifts as an actress seemed to be considerable. Since then her gifts have multiplied and prospered, and Miss Bergman has brought into the theatre a rare purity of spirit. Possibly Joan is an ideal part for her—"clear and clean and honest," as one phrase in the play puts it. The boy's dress becomes her, as do the simplicities of manner. But she transmutes the part into a sentient being by the glow of her spirit as an actress. In her playing, Joan is, as you would expect, a rapturously attractive maiden with pride, grace and a singularly luminous smile. But Miss Bergman adds frankness, force and light that comes out of her own wealth of perception, and hers is the Joan of religious inspiration and fable.

With Romney Brent and Harry Irvine

Richard Watts Jr. in the New York Post:

Although Ingrid Bergman is one of the few celebrated Hollywood girls worthy of the popular enthusiasm bestowed upon her kind, the screaming, pushing mob of movie-mad idiots outside the Alvin Theatre last night made it seem likely that it would be a good thing if all screen stars were barred from the stage forever. Inside the Alvin, however, it became evident that no such edict should apply to Miss Bergman, as she went quietly about the business of bringing that modest but stirring magic of hers to bear on Maxwell Anderson's moderately interesting new play about Joan of Arc. Indeed, the fact that Miss Bergman's return to the stage was the news of the evening has but superficially to do with her eminence in the Beverly Hills hierarchy. The important thing is the quality she imparts to Mr. Anderson's conception of the French heroine.

She is not a remarkably brilliant actress in the technical sense, even though her final scenes are movingly played. What gives her the undoubted distinction she possesses is that strange and inescapable radiance, that quality of shining warmth which add a unique loveliness **and an** irresistible air of lyric simplicity to everything she does.

Louis Kronenberger in PM:

Ingrid Bergman . . . calls forth some of those adjectives that I long ago decided every critic could do very nicely without. She is radiant and enchanting—perhaps not as an actress but simply as a human being. She has a childlike gawkiness which is better than grace, and a beauty that has very little to do with being beautiful, and in a "spiritual" role like her present one, these things are seen at their best.

Joan of Arc at the Stake

1954

CAST

Ingrid Bergman, Valentine Dyall, Harry Hapgood, Eugene Castle, Irving Childs, Michael Greenwood, and a cast of 100, comprising supernumeraries and singers.

CREDITS

Directed by Roberto Rossellini. Opera in eleven scenes by Arthur Honegger. Written by Paul Claudel. Orchestra conducted by Leighton Lucas. Performed at La Scala in Milan; Theatre San Carlos, Palermo; Stockholm Opera, Paris Opera, Barcelona Opera, and at the Stoll Theatre, London. Sung, in various engagements, in Italian, English, Spanish and French. (Opened at the San Carlo Opera House in Naples in 1953. Also heard in a B.B.C. concert performance.)

THE THEME

Classified variously, during its peregrinations throughout Europe in 1953-54, as an opera, semi-opera, oratorio, musical morality play, and musical melodrama, the story follows the career of France's great saint, Joan of Arc, in a blending of choral singing, spoken drama and crowd scenes featuring a number of supernumeraries. Miss Bergman spoke her part throughout.

REVIEW

In The Times (London):

Miss Bergman's is a convincing study of Joan, differentiating the human and the divine, vivid in action, sustained in repose, so that the central figure holds the episodes together without distracting attention from the motley company of those who stage by stage led her to her doom. ... The impressiveness of Claudel's symbolized morality comes through more surely than in the diffraction of the cold light of the concert hall, and the continuity of the eleven scenes is secured by Mr. Rossellini's method of staging and illumination. In essence Honegger's intentions are realized by his treatment, as was apparent at Naples, and they are not obscured in the rough and ready conditions obtaining here. But whereas in the German and Italian opera houses in which it has been performed, it is treated as an opera,

with all the resources of an opera house to give its diverse elements coherence, here it is no more than an aggregate of acting, oratorio and incidental music. What should be an integration is only a synthesis. The crowds on the stage are supers, not singers; the singers are not on the stage but in side boxes, in which sopranos are separated from altos and both from tenors and basses. The tonal balance, which needs the most careful adjustment, especially when Miss Bergman, who has a strong, low-pitched and pleasing voice, is speaking, is uncontrollable by the conductor in such conditions. Mr. Valentine Dyall, who spoke the part in the B.B.C. performance, projected his voice well through the music and was sympathetic and engaging. The singing of Mr. Hapgood was strong and ringing. The choral portions were sung by the Ambrosian singers, but how they sang no one in the front part of the theatre could tell, for the sounds came from north and south, high and low, and never together.

With Jean-Loup Philippe

Tea and Sympathy

1956

CAST

Ingrid Bergman, Jean-Loup Philippe, Yves Vincent, Georges Berger, Simone Paris, Bernard Lajarrige, Guy Sarrazin, Guy Kerner, Bernard Klein, Jean Mondani, Pierre Derone.

CREDITS

A play in three acts and four tableaux by Robert Anderson. French adaptation from the 1953 Broadway hit by Roger-Ferdinand. Presented by Elvire Popesco and Hubert de Malet at the Theatre de Paris, Paris, France. Mise en scène by Jean Mercure. Décor by François Ganeau. The play opened December 2, 1956, closed July 10, 1957, reopened in late September and finally closed October 31, 1957.

THE STORY

Laura Reynolds (Ingrid Bergman) is trapped in an unhappy marriage with Bill Reynolds (Yves Vincent), a teacher, athletic coach and housemaster at a boys' preparatory school. Laura is a sensitive and cultured woman who finds she has little in common with her masculinely assertive and somewhat obtuse spouse. Tom Lee (Jean-Loup Philippe), a fine-grained, sensitive eighteen-year-old, is one of the boys living in her house. Tom does not relate well to his coarser, physically stronger classmates, who style him an "off-horse," call him "sister boy" and comment unkindly on his gentler diversions and artistic bents. Laura finds herself drawn to Tom, and becomes his protectress and chamption against the school, and even against her husband, who shares his pupils' contempt for the retiring and unassertive Tom.

Tom in desperation resolves to visit a town waitress with a loose reputation, thinking that this will shore up his "image" with the school. Laura, overhearing him making the date, tries to divert him, but when Tom, moved and encouraged by her kindness and concern, tries to embrace her, she rebuffs him and he rushes off to the waitress.

Because for Tom it "has to be love," he fails in his attempt to make love to the waitress and when she ridicules him he goes berserk. There is a scandal and Tom's father, Herbert Lee *(Bernard Lajarrige)*, who hitherto had expressed his worries over Tom's "failure to be a regular guy," comes joyfully to the school, feeling that Tom's "scrape" has satisfied his father's foolish concept of "manliness." Bill Reynolds speedily disabuses Mr. Lee of such an impression and tells him Tom failed with the woman. Laura, stung by Bill's cruelty, confronts him, and when she tries to save her marriage with honest talk, real-

With the cast of *Tea and Sympathy* at the time she won the Oscar in 1957. Left to right: Jean-Loup Philippe, Bernard Lajarige, Yves Vincent and Simone Paris.

Miss Bergman accepts ovation from Paris audience.

izes through Bill's reaction that he is sublimating homosexual instincts and does not really love her, preferring the company of his boys. Laura, shorn of all illusions, goes to Tom and, to save the boy's self-concept and heal his emotional wounds, gives herself to him.

REVIEWS

In Combat (French newspaper):

[Miss Bergman] gave full measure to the part and gave an extremely moving performance.

Jean Renoir:

I never saw anything like this performance. Not even Sarah Bernhardt ever did better . . . she can dignify the most trivial film or part.

NOTE

The New York Times' Paris correspondent reported that a packed house of 1500 people cheered Miss Bergman to the rafters, and she took fifteen curtain calls. When she opened, she had barely recovered from an appendicitis operation.

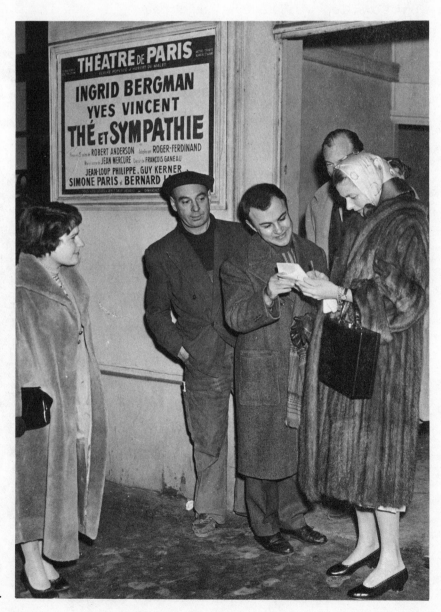

Autographing outside Theatre de Paris.

Hedda Gabler

1962

CAST

Ingrid Bergman, Claude Dauphin, Jean Serbais, Jacques Dacomine and French cast.

CREDITS

A play by Henrik Ibsen. Translation by Gilbert Sigaux. Directed by Raymond Rouleau. Opened at the Theater Montparnasse Gaston Baty, December 10, 1962.

THE STORY

Hedda Gabler, spirited, life-hungry and easily bored, finds herself involved in an unsatisfactory and unfulfilling marriage with a plodding teacher, George Tessman *(Claude Dauphin)*. She realizes that Tessman is never going to win a high station in life, and her contempt for his stuffy, unimaginative ways grows. She sees herself condemned to a marital prison for the rest of her life, and her imperious nature revolts against the prospect.

The sadistic and ironic streaks in her nature come to the fore. She confides carefully-edited aspects of her unhappiness to her staunch friend and admirer, Judge Brack *(Jean Serbais)*, who has lent Tessman the money for his and Hedda's comfortable villa. Hedda's extravagances have forced Tessman to seek a better income, and he is warned by Judge Brack that his chief rival for the government post he is after, is Eilert Lovborg *(Jacques Dacomine)*, a formerly dissipated writer who is now a successful author of a much-discussed book. Lovborg and Hedda had once been intimately involved, but Hedda has long since discarded him. Hedda is jealously resentful because Lovborg has made a success both of his career and his liaison with Thea Elvsted, and she sets out to ruin Lovborg and break the heart of the woman who has inspired his rehabilitation.

She maneuvers Lovborg into resuming his drinking, and when he loses his one and only manuscript of his new book while on a tear, Hedda coolly destroys it. Later she tells Tessman what she has done, claiming that she did it to assure her husband's appointment to the post he and Lovborg both covet.

Lovborg cannot bring himself to tell Thea that he lost the manuscript while drunk, so he pretends to her that he has destroyed it. Hedda then maneuvers the confused and harried Lovborg into killing himself with a gun from the collection of her father, a general. After Lovborg's death, Judge Brack recognizes the gun, and informs Hedda that he knows of her evil purposes. Hedda, now at bay and aware that what she has done will be generally known, kills herself. Tessman and Thea prepare, meanwhile, to salvage the Lovborg manuscript from notes.

REVIEWS

The Paris correspondent in The New York Times:

Of the two alternative conceptions of *Hedda Gabler*—high comedy or high tragedy—the director of the Paris production, Raymond Rouleau, had clearly chosen the second. Given this point of view, the performances by some of France's best-known actors fell into place comfortably enough. Claude Dauphin, in particular, created a very satisfying George Tessman, and both Jean Serbais and Jacques Dacomine scored successes as Judge Brack and Eibert Lovborg. . . . It was in her mime that Miss Bergman scored. Her dumb anguish as she hovered over Lovborg, sharing the agony of his despair, was a brief moment of glory that reminded of her great gifts.

In Newsweek:

More than anything else, actress Ingrid Bergman exudes radiance—a charm totally lacking in the title character of *Hedda Gabler*. Even so, Paris theater critics generally applauded a tenderized Bergman portrayal—in French—of Ibsen's cold, vain, destructive Norwegian beauty.

In The New York Times:

One [Paris] critic said the role did not appear to fit Miss Bergman, despite her Nordic character, because she was "too obviously a nice person to play a wicked woman."

A Month in the Country

1965

CAST

Ingrid Bergman, Michael Redgrave, Fay Compton, Daniel Massey, Max Adrian, Jennifer Hilary, Geoffrey Chater, Peter Pratt. (London Production: Emlyn Williams, Jeremy Brett.)

CREDITS

Directed by Michael Redgrave. Adapted from the play by Ivan Turgenev. Produced in June 1965 at the Yvonne Arnaud Memorial Theatre, Guildford, England. (Moved to the Cambridge

Theatre in London's West End in September 1965.)

THE STORY

The pragmatic-minded Yslaev *(Geoffrey Chater)* lives on his isolated Russian estate with his wife Natalia Petrovna *(Ingrid Bergman)*, a passionate and imaginative woman who is bored and spiritually and emotionally stultified by her prosaic surroundings and recalls wistfully a more exciting and glamorous past. Natalia is also fearful of growing old, and flirts with her husband's friend, Mikhail Rakitin *(Michael Redgrave)*, though his overly polite and tepid attentions bore her.

Enter a magnetic and mercurial young tutor, Alexsei Belaev *(Daniel Massey)*, who has been hired to guide Natalia's son through his studies. Natalia falls in love with Belaev, whose youthful high-spirits and flirtatious ardor rejuvenate her jaded perceptions.

Belaev also flirts with Natalia's beautiful seventeen-year-old ward Vera *(Jennifer Hilary)* and Natalia becomes jealous and petulant. When her jealous rages prove too much for him, Belaev goes back to Moscow. Rakitin also leaves, though Yslaev begs him to remain. Doctor Spigelski, the observant and worldly-wise family friend *(Max Adrian)*, is the only one who really knows what he wants and sees to it that he gets it. He has taught the clumsy neighboring landowner Bolshintsov *(Peter Pratt)* the techniques involved in successfully wooing a young lady, and Vera, embittered and hurt by the departure of Belaev, proves amenable to the old man's proposal of marriage. Natalia is left more lonely, frustrated and bored than ever, her hopes and romantic machinations and elegant self-deceptions having come to nothing.

REVIEWS

In the London Sun:

Emotions chase each other across [Miss Bergman's] mobile face, but all is kept disciplined and controlled. It is a deliberately small performance. (Guildford performance, June, 1965.)

In the Times (London):

Miss Ingrid Bergman and Mr. Michael Redgrave play their parts with a restraint which finely resists the play's temptations. Miss Bergman's performance now has a comic edge which throws the overwritten pathos of the part into more proportionate relief. Mr. Emlyn Williams' doctor is a fine figure of seedy provincial dignity and Mr. Jeremy Brett gives a virtuoso account of a thankless role. (West End performance, September, 1965.)

In The Times (London):

The production would hardly have exerted this special appeal without the presence of Ingrid Bergman, an actress impervious to changes of fashion and whose star quality as an ice goddess with warm human sympathies remains intact after a quarter of a century in the public eye. More than any other performer one can think of, she embodies a stable romantic ideal in the midst of change. (December, 1965.)

With Colleen Dewhurst and Arthur Hill

More Stately Mansions

1967

CAST

Ingrid Bergman, Colleen Dewhurst, Arthur Hill, Fred Stewart, Barry McCallum, Vincent Dowling, Helen Craig, John Marriott, Lawrence Linville, Kermit Murdock.

CREDITS

A play by Eugene O'Neill. Staged by José Quintero. Setting by Ben Edwards. Costumes by Jane Greenwood. Lighting by John Harvey. Production: Wiliam Weaver. Presented by Elliot Martin in association with Center Theatre Group by arrangement with Quinto Productions, Inc. Production associate: Marjorie Martin. Presented at the Broadhurst Theatre on October 31, 1967. (Produced in Stockholm, Sweden, and Salzburg, Austria, in earlier versions, and with Miss Bergman in Los Angeles in September 1967.)

THE STORY

The action takes place between the years 1832 and 1841 and concerns the struggle for the love of Simon Harford (Arthur Hill), scion of a wealthy and aristocratic New England family, that is waged by his wife Sara (Colleen Dewhurst) and his mother Deborah (Ingrid Bergman), the strong-minded and intense matriarch of the family. Chronologically the play derives from the earlier O'Neill play A Touch of the Poet, whose chief protagonist was Con Melody. Con's daughter Sara has married Harford. Harford's mother

With Arthur Hill

With Arthur Hill and Colleen Dewhurst

204

In her dressing room during the run

disapproves of the marriage, feeling that Sara is below both Arthur's and the Harfords' standards. The mother and wife argue discursively over a number of matters, including Simon's one-time Thoreau-ian idealism. To express his concepts of simplistic living, wholesome individualism and scorn of material values, Simon had lived alone in the woods, built his own cabin, supported his needs self-sufficiently, but eventually he had returned to the ambitions and material pursuits of the men around him.

This pursuit of ambition and success have the hearty approval of Deborah, who professes only scorn for Simon's earlier idealism. Sara finds that she is fighting an uphill battle against Deborah for the possession and domination of Simon. She must fight for his loyalty, and even for his love, against his unyielding mother; all three protagonists exhaust their passions and needs upon each other, and at the denouement find that no one has emerged the winner in this contest of needs, passions and long-range aims. All, at last, has been proven vain and futile, and all that remains is to go on as best one can.

REVIEWS

Richard P. Cooke in the Wall Street Journal:

. . . The evening is graced by the reappearance of Ingrid Bergman on the New York stage after a long absence, and, as expected, she is proving to be a warm and welcome presence.

John Chapman in the New York Daily News:

There are fine performances by Ingrid Bergman, Colleen Dewhurst and Arthur Hill in an unholy triangle, and José Quintero, who trimmed

205

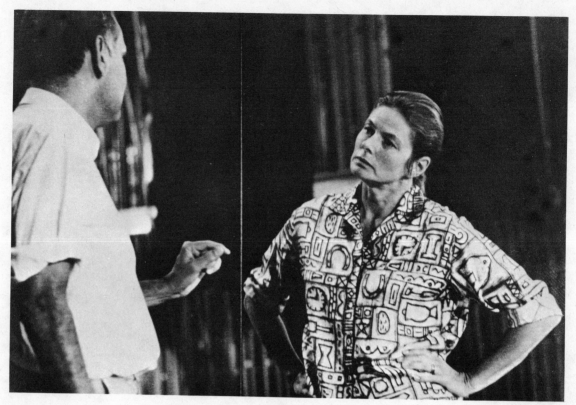

Taking direction from Jose Quintero

and "finished" O'Neill's work, has directed the drama meticulously. Miss Bergman returns to the stage after a long absence, and being an assured and beautiful actress, her presence is welcome. But I still can't fancy her as the greedy grandmother of Hill's and Miss Dewhurst's children.

Richard Watts, Jr., in the New York Post:

Miss Bergman, looking more beautiful than ever, seemed too young and in command of herself to be realistic as the loving and hating mother, but she plays with skill and her characteristic charm.

Clive Barnes in The New York Times:

Ingrid Bergman, returning to the Broadway stage, is a woman so beautiful that she is herself a work of art. But as an actress she is less perfect, and cast as one of O'Neill's archetypal mother figures, she seemed strangely gauche. She trades heavily on her natural charm and, in a sense, her very real inner goodliness (Miss Bergman has only to enter a stage—or, I am sure, a room—and any man with any blood or courtesy in him automatically starts to get up from his seat) but makes less of the strangely disparate character of Deborah Harford than you might have hoped.

Television Appearances

With Rip Torn in *24 Hours in a Woman's Life* **(page 212)**

The Turn of the Screw

NBC-TV, 1959

CAST

Ingrid Bergman, Hayward Morse, Alexandra Wager, Isobel Elsom, Laurinda Barrett, Paul Stevens.

CREDITS

Part of a Tuesday evening series, "Startime," sponsored by Ford. Executive producer, Hubbell Robinson, Jr. Directed by John Frankenheimer. Associate producer-director, Gordon Rigby. Adapted for television by James Costigan from the 1898 novella by Henry James. Music composed and conducted by David Amram. Color. Taped. Telecast October 20, 1959. 90 minutes.

NOTE

For this performance Miss Bergman won TV's Emmy Award.

THE STORY

Two small children, Miles (Hayward Morse)

With Hayward Morse

and Flora *(Alexandra Wager)* are under the influence of the evil spirits of two former servants, now dead, steward Peter Quint and Governess Miss Jessel. Sent to the remote country house in which they live under the care of a housekeeper *(Isobel Elsom)* the new governess *(Ingrid Bergman)* is drawn into a web of supernatural evil brought about partly through her own neurotic predispositions and partly though psychic manifestations. The evil spirits of Quint and Miss Jessel keep appearing to the children. Sometimes the governess sees them and the children do not; sometimes the reverse. The governess is horrified and repelled by the expressions of unmitigated evil on the faces of the apparitions. Watching one night with little Flora, the governess sees one of the spirits, but the girl denies knowledge of the apparition, though her companion is sure the child has seen it.

The children are unusually precocious and birdlike, and the governess, in time, finds their manner, reactions and general aura as chilling as those of the servants' ghosts. At one point, the steward's ghost is swinging a riding crop, and the boy does likewise, motion for motion. Tension mounts as the increasingly hysterical governess realizes that somehow she is fighting a losing game in attempting to "exorcise" the children from their evil influences. The governess' efforts to protect the girl succeed only in arousing the child's fears, and as the black forces close in, the boy, small Miles, dies in the governess' arms while the spectre of the steward looks on through a casement window.

REVIEWS

Rose. in Variety:

To capture Henry James' frightening bout with

Rehearsing with director
John Frankenheimer

the supernatural in all its horrendous overtones is no mean feat, yet James Costigan's vivid and skillful adaptation and John Frankenheimer's always professional direction were equal matches for the extraordinarily fine performances of Miss Bergman and others in the cast. . . . Costigan in his adaptation was faithful to the period piece both in time and style. But the biggest contribution was the warmth and intensity of Miss Bergman's performance.

Jack Gould in The New York Times:

Ingrid Bergman in her first dramatic portrayal in television, gave a performance of shattering and chilling power as the governess. . . . In Miss Bergman's battle to save the souls of two precocious youngsters, whom she sees as possessed by the evil spirits of her predecessors, there was a superb capture of the darkness of the unnatural. In her fluidly mobile face, there was projected the mounting horror of fears and apprehensions better left unspoken. Yet there was also the warmth and sincerity of one who wanted to bolster the youngsters with love and understanding. James Costigan prepared his adaptation with Miss Bergman in mind, and it is well that he did. Except for the rather slow beginning, he built his suspense and tension carefully, and Miss Bergman made them come alive. . . . John Frankenheimer's direction achieved excellent composition. . . . It was Hubbell Robinson, producer of "Startime," who persuaded Miss Bergman to enter the field of dramatic video. For that viewers indeed have reason to be grateful.

Ingrid Bergman on the set

24 Hours in a Woman's Life

CBS-TV, 1961

CAST

Ingrid Bergman, Rip Torn, John Williams, Lili Darvas, Helena de Crespo, Jerry Orbach.

CREDITS

Sponsored by Revlon. Executive producer, Lars Schmidt. Directed by Silvio Narizzano. A television drama by John Mortimer based on a story by Stefan Zweig. Music by George Kleinsinger, conducted by Alfredo Antonini. Taped. Telecast March 20, 1961. Running time, 90 minutes.

THE STORY

Helen Lester (Helena de Crespo) has fallen in love with a young playboy who passes bad checks. She has known him only twenty-four hours. Though the boy, who has been incarcerated for his mischief-making, promises to reform, the girl's straitlaced family is against the match. But Helen's grandmother, Clare (Ingrid Bergman), tells the girl she is free to do as she likes—on condition that she listen to the story of a day in her grandmother's own past, many years before. As a lonely young English widow with nearly grown sons, Clare had visited Monte Carlo and there had encountered Paul (Rip Torn), a spoiled young American of somewhat black and unpredictable moods. At war with his mother and his midwestern background, deeply self-

212

With Rip Torn and director
Silvio Narazzano

destructive by nature, and given to a compulsion to gambling, Paul wins Clare's sympathy—and finally her love—and she tries to stem his self-destructive pursuits. Paul professes love for her, and otherwise leads her on, while continuing to gamble obsessively. Eventually Clare pays his enormous gambling debts, asking only that he quit gambling forever. But Paul, having squandered Clare's money, deserts her and Clare, a sadder but wiser woman, withdraws permanently into a life of reclusive dignity.

REVIEWS

Jack Gould in The New York Times:

The multitudinous admirers of Ingrid Bergman were put to a rather stringent loyalty test last night. The gracious actress appeared on Channel 2 in a drama entitled "24 Hours In A Woman's Life" and all in all, it was one terribly long day. The taped vehicle chosen for the Swedish star's second major appearance on the home screen unfortunately reflected an excessive generosity in matters of narrative scope and diversity of interpretation. In the play there were discernible traces of Stefan Zweig, "Intermezzo" and "Our Gal Sunday." In the playing and direction there appeared to be a determined endeavor to reach an accommodation between the Actors Studio and a J. J. Shubert operetta. Presumably the end product was designed to qualify as a "woman's story" which would drain the distaff viewers of the last iota of emotion. At least, in a hilarious juxtaposition of one of the middle commercials, the cosmetics sponsor offered a hopeful cross-reference to the evening's "fire and ice." But from a more detached perspective, it was hard to down the thought that a more apt description of the night's events would have included mention of snow that had melted. The television drama was concerned with a lovely middleaged widow of striking charm and carriage qualities that meant Miss Bergman was not ill-cast in the slightest. Indeed, to see the actress in closeup was not an inconsiderable reward in itself. But the story was ridiculous. . . . Miss Bergman's international fan club can only regret the burden she had to carry. The characters of the widow and young man, played by Rip Torn, relied al-

With Rip Torn during a lull in the taping

most entirely on suffering of the dullest sort; they never had the dimension of people to make their unhappiness come to life. Under the circumstances, the actress, humanly enough, succumbed to interpretive exaggerations in hopes of compensating for the sterility of plot and dialogue. Mr. Torn had a night of giddy introspection and managed to make the American seem bereft of qualities inviting minimum pity. Silvio Narizzano, who recently did such a brilliant job in directing "No Exit" last night seemed to have mislaid the knob turning off the "Stream of Consciousness" tedium.

In Variety:

The Madison Avenue scuttlebutt is that once the scrapped tape, the retakes and the struck sets were toted up, the initially projected $275,000 sponsor-tab perilously approached the half-million production mark. . . . But for what? It's conceivable that even the daytime soap opera impresarios would think twice before inflicting such old-hat tempoed cornpone on the viewer. . . . (The teleplay) had perhaps the most gifted videogenic personality extant in Miss Bergman . . . (her) beauty was at times breathtaking. She had style, warmth and class . . . but for what? . . . the stereotyped cliches were in abundance in the unfolding of this ebbing-from-joy-to-tragedy Zweig trifle. . . . Rip Torn tried in vain to alternately capture the incorrigible weakness of the character and the youth and charm that would make a woman like Bergman fall for him.

With her three leading men: Trevor Howard, Sir Michael Redgrave and (front) Sir Ralph Richardson.

Hedda Gabler

CBS-TV, 1963

CAST

Ingrid Bergman, Michael Redgrave, Ralph Richardson, Trevor Howard, Dilys Hamlett, Ursula Jeans, Beatrice Varley.

CREDITS

Produced by David Susskind, Lars Schmidt and Norman Tutherford. Directed by Alex Segal. A television adaptation by Phil Reisman Jr. of an Eva LeGallienne translation of a play by Henrik Ibsen. Taped. Telecast September 20, 1963 after an earlier B.B.C. presentation in England. Running time, 90 minutes.

THE STORY

Hedda Gabler is the beautiful, spirited and life-hungry daughter of a general. Autocratic, self-involved and easily bored, she finds herself trapped in a marriage with a dull professor, George Tessman (Michael Redgrave) whose career prospects she now realizes she has overrated. After a honeymoon abroad, during which George has spent most of his time researching, Hedda gives rein to her diabolically sadistic and ironical nature. She confides discreetly edited aspects of her boredom and restlessness to her friend and admirer, Judge Brack (Ralph Richardson) to win his sympathy. Hedda's luxurious tastes have increased Tessman's expenses and he hopes to meet them by obtaining a government appointment.

Judge Brack warns Tessman that his chief rival for the appointment is Eilert Lovborg (*Trevor Howard*), a successful author, once a dissipated roué who had enjoyed an intimate friendship with Hedda. Though Hedda had abandoned Lovborg in the past, she is now fretfully jealous because Lovborg has made a success of his relationship with Thea Elvsted (*Dilys Hamlett*) who inspired his writing success. Hedda sets out to regress Lovborg into the hard-drinking failure he once was, and when by accident the only manuscript of his new book comes into her hands, she destroys it.

Later she tells her shocked husband of her act, giving the excuse that Lovborg was his chief career threat. Lovborg, ashamed to admit to Thea that he had lost the manuscript while drunk, tells her that he has destroyed it. Lovborg, distraught, decides on suicide and Hedda aids and abets him by presenting him with one of her father's pistols and urging him to die nobly. Judge Brack, after Lovborg's suicide, recognizes the general's pistol and confronts Hedda with his knowledge of her evil designs. Hedda, realizing that the truth will eventually out, shoots herself, while Tessman and Thea are preparing to reconstruct the Lovborg book from notes he has left.

REVIEWS

Jack Gould in The New York Times:

The Ibsen work on tape, a project of the indefatigable David Susskind and the British Broadcasting Corporation, is a shimmering paradox. In the context of the theatrical vacuity that so often blights the domestic channels, the production's ambitions alone were a cause for rejoicing—a pearl of intent amid all the resignation to mediocrity. A viewer starved for substance had reason to be thankful for the opportunity to witness a major star's approach to a classic portrait in the literature of the theatre. Mr. Susskind's instincts are noble. Moreover, for the legions of Bergman fans, the 90 minutes on Channel 2 may have been fully rewarding by the mere fact of her presence, by the face and figure that so easily can erase concern for all other relevancies. Such pleasure, the record should show, extended to many sections of the British press last year. But what of Hedda, the embodiment of evil and destruction, who generates an ascending tension that should be almost unbearable? As luck would have it, she was the pallid one last night, stunning as only Miss Bergman can be, but so hesitatingly involved in the dark proceedings that the spectator never felt an irresistible pull toward full emotional commitment. In the modern theatre, *Hedda Gabler* poses many difficulties but what saves the play is the sadistic drive that Hedda finds release for her frustration and boredom until she is finally and tragically devoured by her own malevolence. The weakness of the woman Miss Bergman realized. But the overriding passion and restlessness of the prisoner, unable to accept the lifetime sentence to the home and to the mores of her time, was never felt on either side of the screen. On television Hedda was too much the suffering heroine of the cinema and not enough the Ibsen animal of cold cunning and temperament who savors her evil acts. Alex Segal's direction had the technical facility for which it is noted but missing was a strong point of view toward the Ibsen work which could have brought Hedda into compelling focus. In a presentation where marquee considerations are of such great importance, however, a viewer cannot divine a director's difficulties, among them his helplessness in the face of middle commercials. They did not contribute to the maintenance of the Ibsen mood.

Rose. in Variety:

This was a handsomely mounted Hedda and under Segal's skillful direction (it) was endowed with warmth and vigor. In fact, the vitality was such that the presentation captured successfully the reality of the theatre. But primarily what distinguished this "Hedda" were the performances by the four leads and notably that by Miss Bergman. . . . The fascinating character (of Hedda) was brought to life and understanding. Always the cameras took advantage of her beautiful and intelligent face and the Bergman voice is as mellifluous and of as exquisite a timbre as always. Ralph Richardson, Trevor Howard and Michael Redgrave . . . gave finely-etched, sensitive performances.

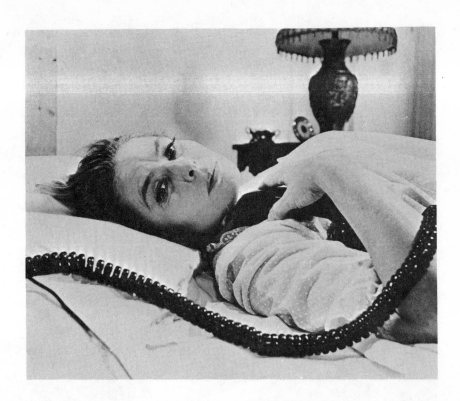

The Human Voice

ABC-TV, 1967

CAST

Ingrid Bergman.

CREDITS

Produced by David Susskind and Lars Schmidt. A Stage 67 Presentation. Directed by Ted Kotcheff. Adapted for TV by Clive Exton from an idiomatic translation by Carl Wildman of a story by Jean Cocteau. Telecast in U.S. via Rediffusion, from an October 1966 tape made in London. U.S. Telecast May 4, 1967. Running time, 50 minutes.

NOTE

At the time the telecast was shown, Miss Bergman told the press, "I chose this play as a tribute to the memory of my friend, Jean Cocteau." The French playwright had first written the play in 1930 in the form of a telephone conversation.

THE STORY

Miss Bergman, who is the only character in the teleplay (unless you could term the man on the other end of the telephone, and the telephone itself, her co-stars) plays a middle-aged woman who has lost her younger lover to a girl he has married. She waits impatiently and anxiously for him to phone. Their lines get crossed. They get cut off. She calls him, to find that he has been lying about being home. Actually he is in a restaurant. They talk several times during the teleplay, and the lady runs the gamut of emotions: alternately tender and loving, then reproachful and bitter. She voices regret for lost love and lost youth; she indulges in flights of self-pity and self-reproach; she comes on as the woman wronged. Though she knows she is not going to win back her lover, she is trying to loosen herself gently from the attachment, being aware that suicide may be the only alternative

to the lifegiving force that her love for this younger man represents. The author, Jean Cocteau, had described the character Miss Bergman is playing here as "a mediocre victim, in love from beginning to end." It is obvious that there can be no "happy ending" to the situation presented, filled as it is with heartbreak and the finalities of despair—nor is a "happy ending" foisted on the viewer.

REVIEWS

In the New York Daily News:

[Miss Bergman] once more proved her quality. Tender and whimsical, gay and tragic, by turns hers was a performance of remarkable virtuosity. She created magic . . . and touched the heart.

In Variety:

The Human Voice is a tour de force for an actress, and Ingrid Bergman gave a formidable display of passionate despair, showing a side to her talent not often vouchsafed by the movies. Cocteau's famous little play, with its single character and claustrophobic set of one, littered room, accorded well with TV's ability to put emotions in closeup, and Ted Kotcheff's inventive direction ensured that monotony didn't set in. He isolated details and moods with splendid flair, using swift cross-cutting from camera to camera to give a sense of movement. But it was Miss Bergman's show, and with the slight reser-

vation that she is perhaps too sensible a personality to give way to a broken heart so abjectly, she triumphed. . . . It is the fault of the play that its ingenuity got in the way of its sym-

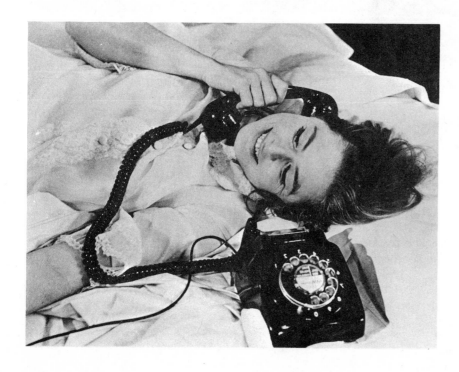

the warmth and skill of a considerable actress.

In Newsday:

The drama was a fertile showcase for Ingrid Bergman's considerable talents . . . Miss Bergman made lavish use of her emotional range. Acting with, to and for a telephone that rang periodically to reunite her with her lover—and keep her tied to life—Miss Bergman was a veritable stream of anguish.

Bob Williams in the New York Post:

Ingrid Bergman did everything she imaginably could last night on ABC in trying to sustain interest for an hour in the portrayal of a shattered middle-aged woman trying desperately to win back her lover by telephone. However [the teleplay] became a monologue of monotony, despite the camera play and the usual sponsor-interruptions. Director Ted Kotcheff played vigorously with his cameras in the London production but in vain. The expensive ABC "Stage 67" Hour seemed inadvisable at least.

In Christian Science Monitor:

Unfortunately that Jean Cocteau telephone play which kept Ingrid Bergman alone on the screen for an unrelieved hour was a "tour de forced" for her.

pathy, but Miss Bergman overcame it by a versatile, deeply-felt study of a woman on the brink of suicide, that last love being, it seemed, her final attempt to find happiness. . . . The hour made a memorable contribution to the fall schedules, and records at the top of her form

The Face of
INGRID BERGMAN
Through the Years

224